Prickles and the bubbles

Ekta Bera

 pencil

ISBN 978-93-5610-772-4
© Ekta Bera 2022
Published in India 2022 by Pencil

A brand of

One Point Six Technologies Pvt. Ltd.
123, Building J2, Shram Seva Premises,
Wadala Truck Terminal, Wadala (E)
Mumbai 400037, Maharashtra, INDIA
E connect@thepencilapp.com
W www.thepencilapp.com

Author biography

Hi, I am Ekta Bera based in India. I am a researcher, writer, a designer, web developer and the author of "Prickles and the bubbles." Mostly, I love putting my own experiences into words to connect with humans and moments that matter.

CONTENTS

Introduction

Adwika, the name has always been fascinating to me. I'd been thinking that if I ever get a chance to change my name, I would change it to Adwika instead of Ekta. No! It doesn't mean I absolutely hate my current name, it's just that I like Adwika's name somewhere a bit more, and more than my current name! But unfortunately, I probably won't get any scope to change my name. Besides, I realized, I still can do something about it. To my future daughter. Yes! I am going to call her Adwika for the rest of her life. It is kind of funny that I am still unmarried when I am planning my daughter's name. Anyways, I know, I will get married to a beautiful man, and have a daughter. I know I will have one day!

I am still figuring out why I like those tongue twisters complex names when I already have a much simpler name that doesn't even cost my energy to call upon. Well, some things aren't just reasonable, they have to be accepted the way they are.

Just like life, certain things happen to us that we control, but more than that, there are certain, uncertain things that can't be controlled. Trust me, that is the beauty of it, the uniqueness of it.

Because life is a journey and a journey can't be as smooth as you can slip off. It has to be perfect with those imperfections so that you get a better grip of it, a better understanding, and a way better perception of it. That's life, and that's about living life. It's tough, but it's beautiful. My journey till now has not been at all easy. I was not the perfect person that everyone dreams about, and I still am not the perfect one. I have flaws… So damn many flaws. I made mistakes. I failed almost at everything, as a daughter, a sister, a friend, a student, and everywhere else. I hated having such a life. I hated myself, everything, and everybody who was there in my life. It was getting so heavy inside that I felt so defeated and wanted to end everything, whatever I had. But just like "Calm comes after a storm", I survived. I survived that storm and the moment I decided to live, I started understanding that the beauty of living lies in all the experiences, no matter what it is, good or bad. Life shouldn't have to be perfect, it's all those imperfections that make it perfect and beautiful.

It doesn't matter what life throws at you; it's always about you, and how you manage it is the only thing that matters. Furthermore, if you start embracing everything and analyzing it, trust me, there is no more lovely feeling than this. Having a perfect life with imperfections is the most precious thing someone can have.

Even though it was late in my life, when I realized the imperfections and their beauty, I couldn't help but fall for them. The next thing I knew, I was in love with whatever I had. I began to appreciate myself, my life, the people in it, and everything else around me.

I know everyone has a different journey, different experiences, and different visions of their lives. Still, it would make sense if I tell my future kid about my experiences so that it would be easier for her to embrace everything open-handed and also to work on our bond of friendship rather than a parent-child relationship. And after all, a great bond begins with a great conversation.

Isn't it wonderful to tell your kid about your whole life, your mistakes, your commitments, your imperfections, and your honesty?

Delete Created with Sketch.

Adwika, the name has always been fascinating to me. I'd been thinking that if I ever get a chance to change my name, I would change it to Adwika instead of Ekta. No! It doesn't mean I absolutely hate my current name, it's just that I like Adwika's name somewhere a bit more, and more than my current name! But unfortunately, I probably won't get any scope to change my name. Besides, I realized, I still can do something about it. To my future daughter. Yes! I am going to call her Adwika for the rest of her life. It is kind of funny that I am still unmarried when I am planning my daughter's name. Anyways, I know, I will get married to a beautiful man, and have a daughter. I know I will have one day!

I am still figuring out why I like those tongue twisters complex names when I already have a much simpler name that doesn't even cost my energy to call upon. Well, some things aren't just reasonable, they have to be accepted the way they are.

Just like life, certain things happen to us that we control, but more than that, there are certain, uncertain things that can't be controlled. Trust me, that is the beauty of it, the uniqueness of it.

Because life is a journey and a journey can't be as smooth as you can slip off. It has to be perfect with those imperfections so that you get a better grip of it, a better understanding, and a way better perception of it. That's life, and that's about living life. It's tough, but it's beautiful. My journey till now has not been at all easy. I was not the perfect person that everyone dreams about, and I still am not the perfect one. I have flaws… So damn many flaws. I made mistakes. I failed almost at everything, as a daughter, a sister, a friend, a student, and everywhere else. I hated having such a life. I hated myself, everything, and everybody who was there in my life. It was getting so heavy inside that I felt so defeated and wanted to end everything, whatever I had. But just like "Calm comes after a storm", I survived. I survived that storm and the moment I decided to live, I started understanding that the beauty of living lies in all the experiences, no matter what it is, good or bad. Life shouldn't have to be perfect, it's all those imperfections that make it perfect and beautiful.

It doesn't matter what life throws at you; it's always about you, and how you manage it is the only thing that matters. Furthermore, if you start embracing everything and analyzing it, trust me, there is no more lovely feeling than this. Having a perfect life with imperfections is the most precious thing someone can have.

Even though it was late in my life, when I realized the imperfections and their beauty, I couldn't help but fall for them. The next thing I knew, I was in love with whatever I had. I began to appreciate myself, my life, the people in it, and everything else around me.

I know everyone has a different journey, different experiences, and different visions of their lives. Still, it would make sense if I tell my future kid about my experiences so that it would be easier for her to embrace everything open-handed and also to work on our bond of friendship rather than a parent-child relationship. And after all, a great bond begins with a great conversation.
Isn't it wonderful to tell your kid about your whole life, your mistakes, your commitments, your imperfections, and your honesty?

Delete Created with Sketch.

I. prickles on my way.

prickles.

Everybody has some or the other problem in their lives. No matter how big or small it may be… A problem is a problem. But still, the bigger problem with some people is not facing them.

Imagine a marathon runner who just finished his race within two and a half hours. Appreciable, right? And he is smiling right now because he just achieved his goal. He is smiling through his sweat, through pain, and through all the hurdles he had to go through. He is cheering for the efforts he put not just on this day, but every single day. He knew this was only possible when he put in those extra efforts every single day. But was that easy? Not at all! After all, he is a human, he might not have the same physical or mental state every day, but he knew in this process, that only his efforts matter that he had to put every day. He knew that if he puts some extra effort into building his strength, he can achieve his goal with less effort. He knew that these hurdles today will make him stronger for tomorrow.

Each step forward counts as a better step for tomorrow.

Not just for a marathon runner, it is the same for every individual and for every goal. Everyone might not have the same struggle but everyone does have a struggle behind their success.

And that's why I believe, struggles are the most important part of success. After all, a satisfying success is when you earn it. It's when you work for it.

I have a very long-term relationship with my problems. Be it with my family, friendship, academics, health, or anything else, I had problems with everything and everyone in my life. Well, I had to face problems. And that's how my journey was not at all easy.

But each time I face a problem, I know I am digging out what I am made for, I am figuring out what I am responsible to give back to my life.

That's how my problems, yesterday's problems, and my prickles define what I am today, and what I am meant for tomorrow.

virginity with friendships.

While growing up, a phase comes in everyone's life called school life. It is considered to be the golden phase because it really is! School life is the most crucial, the most innocent, and the most important part of everyone's life.

Be it education, friendships, or match-making, everything happens in one place, the school. It is a place for making memories. Memories to be remembered forever. And I made several of them. However, I was not that lucky to have the experience of the last one… Match-making.

Well, the experiences I had in my school weren't something that can be called happy memories because they weren't. Whatever experiences I had, especially with friendships, are more than memories, they are lessons.

When I was young, my mom used to say "You are too innocent to survive in this world". I didn't understand it at first, but when I did, I knew she was right. I was really innocent, especially when trusting people, I meant friendship.

When I was in my first school, I had a friend named Soumya, she was kind of sweet, and with whom I used to spend most of my time, at least till the time I was caught in the crossfires because of her stupidity. She made me turn into a mediator, exchanging her notes, love letters, and other items for a boy who used to be my neighbor, and the boy reciprocated. Everything was going swimmingly until my mother discovered those notes in my school bag.

In general, my mother is very sweet and generous. She doesn't even interfere with my stuff, but when she found those letters in my bag, her instant reaction was nothing but firing questions after questions. I know, she misunderstood me. She thought those were for me. But "how should I tell you, mom? I've never been so lucky."

Wait! The worst part is yet to come. Soumya's mother called my mother yelling "Why is your daughter doing all these? Ask her not to dare to do anything like that in the future."

Just a true friend thing… She was caught on the same day I was caught with her stuff. Seriously? But she still could do something about it. She would rather tell her mother the entire truth from beginning to end, but why? Why would she do that? After all, it was me on the other end, so…

My mother didn't allow me to go to school that day, instead gave me her best lecture on the cruel world to date. She'd tell me not to be so innocent that other people take advantage of me. Nonetheless, her words persuaded me and I was convinced that I won't be trusting people from now on. But…

When I moved to Visakhapatnam for my intermediate studies, it was the first time I went away from home alone to a hostel. Because I was already separated from my family, I had no choice but to rely on those around me. It was a fantastic opportunity to try new things, particularly making friends, which I was already very good at. I did the same, making many new friends and being fortunate to have a roommate from the same hometown as mine. Nikita is the daughter of my father's colleague.

I was overjoyed and relieved because I had found someone

from my hometown. It's because when you're not at home, people from the same area can better connect with one another. So the next step was to strengthen our bond. We began sharing everything from our most ridiculous gossip to our most personal information. After a few days had passed, she told me about her boyfriend. But, since I didn't have any, how could I tell her my story?

I'd never met him or seen a photograph of him except for the fact I knew that her boyfriend is from our hometown, how they are madly in love with each other, and how far they could go in their relationship. We didn't have our cellphones with us. Because of course, we were not allowed to have that inside campus. And after we came back from there and I went to college, I hadn't had any contact with anyone till that time. So I didn't have any idea about anyone and neither did about her. Did I not tell you? I had no cellphone, so obviously, I couldn't contact anyone.

I know, you must be thinking why would I not meet her when we were in the same city? That's because… I don't know. I'm weird.

All thanks to the massive Facebook, which has helped many people find their missing loved ones, of which I was one. When I started college, I got my first cellphone, and I made my first Facebook account. Others saw it as a match-making platform, but I saw it as a way to reconnect with old friends I had lost touch with after graduating from high school. I found several of them, including Nikita.

Thank you, God! At the very least, I can learn about what's going on in the lives of my friends. If not all, at least Nikita, because we were apparently very close friends by the time. We began by saying "Hi" on Facebook

Messenger, and after exchanging numbers, she sent me a picture. Man! Isn't it true that at least one person should have a conversation about the picture, or that the person to whom you are sending the picture should be aware of it? But, as I told you, we were that close.

When I asked about that picture, she told me it was her boyfriend's. She'd ask me next, "Remember? I told you about him." That's around two years back. But I have a great memory. I instantly replied, "Yes yes, I do!" And then we had a pretty good time conversing.

After a few days, she told me she wanted me to be added to a WhatsApp group she had created only for the three of us.

Three!

Nikita, Nikita's boyfriend, and I "Okay!" "I said. Then we talked for a few days, and as our bond grew stronger, Nikita asked me to plan a meeting. It was a more casual meeting, and she had a condition. She asked me not to tell her father about her boyfriend, who is also accompanying her. "Wait, what? Your boyfriend?"

Umm… I was not prepared for that. But what could I possibly say to her instead of Okay?

We three met for a movie and had fun eating outside. But soon, I realized the plan was not to meet me. It was for them because the two of them couldn't meet for a couple of months, so they had to plan something that worked, and she used me as a plan.

Man! My life… That, however, was not the climax.

One day, in the evening, when I was about to open my book to study, my cell phone started ringing. It was an unknown number. Obviously, I picked up the call and wondered who was speaking on the other side. It was a male voice warning me not to introduce any boys to Nikita. "Wait, where does that come from? And who the hell is he?"

When I asked, "Who are you?" He said, "I am Nikita's fiance." I told him the truth but obviously, he didn't believe me and started yelling at me more. I thought let it be! Why waste my energy proving a point when the other person is not even ready to listen to it?

After that incident, I deleted and blocked her and her boyfriend's numbers. But a few days down, Nikita's boyfriend called me up with another number, wondering if I was doing good. The time when I strictly warned him not to call me for any reason, I could hear him weeping. I asked him, "What happened?" He said, "Your friend is getting married." I said, "I already know that." Then he told me his side of the story.

She and her boyfriend were playing hide and seek from their families, but how long could one hide the truth? One day, Nikita was caught meeting her boyfriend in her room. When she was asked multiple questions about her boyfriend, she neither looked to her right nor left and told a completely different story about where Ekta was the villain. "Ekta did everything." "Ekta made her into that boy, and nevertheless, she never wanted to meet him."

I felt so bad for her boyfriend till the moment he asked me to be his girlfriend next. What!?

I can't do that. It's true that I didn't have a boyfriend, but I can't even imagine him being my boyfriend either. No... Never! I blocked his new number too.

My goodness!

I felt really sorry for myself and for my mom who had given me the whole day's lecture on how not to be so innocent.

Sorry, mom, I made another mistake. And now onwards, I promise you, I won't be repeating the same mistake again.

Well, it's the future that no one knows about… You don't even have an idea where it would take you to. And just like I spoke about the future which no one can tell, I was unaware that I would make the same mistake of believing people. Honestly, if I could know about my future, I would definitely not do that, and of course, I wouldn't have to feel and say sorry to my mom, also for myself.

When I first started college, I was disappointed because it was nothing like what I had imagined. My college was not the stereotypical college that Bollywood has painted in our minds. It was more like a school than a college, where we had to carry bags with notebooks for all of the subjects and books for it, as well as the big practical notebooks for all of the subjects and some stationery. Yeah! I know, these are far too many for a college, but we didn't have anything else to do here. So, with those heavy books on my shoulders and the heavy lessons from people along the way, I did nothing but enjoy whatever it was. On this journey, I met a few people and lost touch with a few others. It took me three long years to realize that it was okay; I made a lot of memories there, even if the majority of them were not the positive ones.

And that's how Ranchi became the city of memories for me. Although it is widely known for its waterfalls all around it. The sweet, and the sour, it takes all the best memories of my life. I still talk about Ranchi being the best city I have ever seen in my entire life. It not only allowed me to explore my academic side and get my Bachelor's degree, but also made me learn life lessons, and probably the best ones of all time.

Did I tell you that our college was exclusively for females? Yes! It was a women's college. And I went to that college not because my parents wouldn't trust me to study in a co-ed college where I'd probably waste my academic career after a boy, but because our college was the second-best college in town after Xavier's, which had closed admissions by the time I decided to do my Bachelors' from Ranchi.

Despite the fact that I have had very little male interaction in my entire life, I had three men on my list. Because they couldn't be from my college, the two of them were from my childhood school, and the third one was a little different. During my intermediate studies, I met him through one of my classmates. But, as I previously stated, I didn't have a cellphone to communicate with anyone until I arrived at college. On the other hand, it was all thanks to social media, where I found most of my lost ones, and where I found the third boy on my list… Did I mention his name?

Saurav. He was from West Bengal and could speak Bengali too. Oh my God! Again the same. I found one with whom I could connect better. Because I did tell you, I was away from home, and of course like people connect with each other better than anyone else.

And that's how he became the closest among all others. It was more than just small talk. We were so close that we even could share about our families without any hesitation. I shared everything with him but I didn't care whether it was the same from his end too.

Starting with a "Good morning" text to a "Good night" call, our bond evolved stronger. I know, you would be thinking, he must be my boyfriend? Well, I really don't know whether he was my boyfriend or a true friend. I don't know whether it was a relationship or was just a true friendship. I don't know whether he felt the same way but I felt some real connection with him. And I am sure it can't be called a true friendship because… It wasn't in the way it turned out to be.

I believe, a relationship with a person is defined by the trust you have and I must say it was a kind of blind trust from my side. Man! In his every high and low, I was there for him. I supported him in every aspect I could, emotionally and financially too. And when you can go to that extent for a person, that implies that you are true to your emotions, and your feelings are genuine. But the other person… As I said that my feelings and my support blind-eyed me and made me unable to see the truth.

I know, I was really stupid!

Our messages, calls, our bond, everything was growing bit by bit, and we were… Same as we were on the very first day when we met. Well, I am talking about the day I found him on Facebook, the day when we never turn back after that. And obviously, we never met in person. Like that, five years down and we only have seen our bond deepening over time.

Did I tell you I only had three boys and a few girls on my list? I even deleted my Facebook account after finding Saurav, thinking I wouldn't need it anymore. Because I always prefer quality over quantity, I reasoned that Saurav alone would be worth hundreds of my friends. So it's best not to be on Facebook. It was entirely my idea; he had no idea I'd ever do something like that in my life, but yes! I did.

Just after a month or so… I was bored of not being on Facebook. So, I decided to create another account, because why not when it's free?

There are very few times when I make a decision really quickly, and this was one of a kind. So, I didn't get any time to tell this to Saurav, unlike all the other things. And like so, I was scrolling through it when my finger on the screen stopped by a profile. The name on the account said "Aryan Sarkar" but the display picture…

A huge shock! I don't know why it happens to me? I really don't have any idea. The picture had a face, I know for eight long years. It was none other than Saurav. But why the hell does he have a different name?

With all the curiosity and confusion, I opened that profile. Man! It had 100s of pictures posted, and almost every picture he had already sent me, and the account has been active since 2011.

Trust me, at first, I thought it might be some fake account and someone might be misusing his picture on their profile. I already planned to speak about this to him. But as I said, there are very few things that I do really quickly. And I am grateful that I decided to check on the profile first before speaking directly to him about this.

Tell me one thing, even if someone is misusing your pictures, he can't have all the pictures of you posted on the wall that you have in your gallery. No! I am not a cyber security expert or some sort of detective but thank God I at least had the common sense at that time.

I didn't know how to do this? I really didn't know. I was so blank. I felt cheated. The person with whom I was talking for the last five years, doesn't even exist. Everything he had told me about his name, family, the place he lives, even his birth date… All lies.

Now, you must be asking about my friend, I meant our mutual friend during my intermediate studies through whom I met Saurav… Oh sorry! Aryan. That friend of ours got married post intermediate so, yeah! We barely talk once or twice in the decades.

Well, at that moment all I needed was support, someone I could tell everything to, and a person who won't even judge me. But… As I said, I was completely detached from all other friends of mine after I met Saurav so, I didn't even have anyone this close to speaking about what I am feeling. That night and several others were traumatic for me.

I was a college-going girl, I know. But, I wasn't at all prepared for these things yet.

I still remember, after everything that happened that night, the time was around 10:20 or 30 when I thought I should call him once and let him know that enough of this hide and seek. Now it's time for the truths. I was thinking, "why would someone do that to me? And after all, why me all the time?"

I grabbed my cell phone and dialled his number. He was one of those who loves to sleep, the only time when he doesn't bother about anything else. By the time I called him, he must be sleeping because he didn't notice it was me on the other side. He replied with a croaky voice "Hello". I didn't waste any moment and simply asked him, "Aryan Sarkar?" He replied, "Yes…" and that was the moment I couldn't hold my tears rolling down my eyes. I said "Ekta this side." "Why did you do this to me?" Soon, his voice returned to normal, as if he was shocked when all his lies were caught. He didn't say anything. Clearly, what would he speak after all of these? That call lasted 38 minutes that night, and it was the last one I made before deciding not to contact him again. Neither he nor I said anything; it was all blank and silent.

He was literally a cheat and as much as I am disappointed after trusting him once in my life, I owe him for learning not to trust anyone else again.

My mom must be proud as I really have learned not to trust anyone. I believed that the world is really cruel. And there is really no room for your innocence. I wish I could have learned it earlier, but yeah! Better late than never!

And there are no surprises! Why do I have so few friends that I can count on my fingers? Simply because I am afraid of being cheated again in the future.

locked horns.

I am an outspoken extremist. And I absolutely despise it… Everything about it. You see, the problem with being an extremist is that if I feel strongly about something, I will express it, and then I am willing to go the extra mile for it. But if I don't feel like it, I won't even look at it and will simply walk away. Although this is a positive trait of mine, it is also one of my greatest weaknesses.

And most of it… I have struggled through. Precisely, the most difficult chapter of life.

You know, I grew up watching movies where the hero is always there for the girl, protecting her from any trouble she gets herself into. At the time, I imagined my life to be like one of those girls in a movie. Man! Place one foot on the ground. There will be no one to protect you every time you get into trouble in real life.

It's strange how one moment you loved being yourself, with the people around you, and everything else, but the next you have to unlove everything and forget everything you once had. It's extremely difficult to forget things that were once the most important in your life.

I've already told you that life is a journey, but did I tell you that you'll meet a lot of new people along the way? Some will leave when their destination arrives, while others may promise to travel until you arrive, but what if a storm hits and your ship flips? Destroyed! Everything… Your entire journey.

Then you'll have to restart it all over again. I wish I had known this truth much sooner in my life. I just wish I'd known that not every moment would be as joyful as this one. Today may be a bright sunny day, but tomorrow may not be so; it may rain, so I should bring my own umbrella.

In most of my memories, I know my mother to be the strongest woman in the entire world. She went through several surgeries on her body but I don't know how she gets the courage to smile through all the pain. I have seen her smiling on the day her hysterectomy happened. She had carried both me and my brother and had to have C-sections both times. And God! Again she had to get that womb out of her with an operation. In those years she had to have another operation, a stone. Man! Her life is just…

She is a ray of inspiration in my life. I am most inspired to become stronger physically. But mentally… I guess I am still weak in this. I was literally vulnerable when it came to tackling emotions. And am still not an expert in tackling them, but certainly, I turned myself to be a better one.

I was in my second last semester at the University when I caught myself struggling with myself, and my emotions. I felt defeated. I felt as if this is the end when I was being cheated by Saurav. Everything was in my head, I'd been thinking the entire time, "I wish, I could do this" I wish I could do that… I wish… I wish… And I wish…. But I couldn't do any of it. All I could do was either lose myself bit by bit or restart everything.

I was so deeply buried in the weight of those regrets that I couldn't even see above it. I couldn't see the other side of it. Although I was pretending to be very strong in front of people, I wasn't! I was smiling but I was not happy.

Then there was a time when I just hated being around the

mirror. I hated looking into it. I hated clicking pictures and being around people. And the most unbelievable thing, I hated music. I mean, seriously? I didn't even notice but slowly I started hating myself. I couldn't sleep at night, because as soon as I tried, my mind used to get driven by all those oceans of thoughts. I was struggling with thoughts, overthinking, and whatnot?

More than that, I recall that night, after dinner, when I jumped into my bed and tried to sleep. I tossed and turned for three hours. That was something I struggled with earlier as well, but that night was a little longer. I got out of bed and went to the bathroom, where I sat on the floor. It was getting so heavy inside that I realized there had to be an end to this. All I could think about was how to put an end to everything. And I thought this would be the last night. It was really too much for me. All I could hear in my room was the sound of the ceiling fan, which was even more pathetic than it sounds. It was late, so everyone was sleeping by that point, and I honestly didn't have the courage to wake anyone up and tell them what I was going through.

While I had so much rush of thoughts in my head, the first thing I grabbed was my cell phone, which I tossed to the floor. And I must say… If I survived today, it was entirely due to my cell phone. When I shoved my phone, the screen turned on, and I have to tell you… Within that millisecond, it turned out to be something else.

Just a moment earlier, I wanted to end this. And now… I didn't. I saw that picture on my screen, my family's picture. There were four of us; me, my mom, my dad, and my brother. It was quite candid. And thanks to my cousin who had framed those four happy faces. As soon as my eyes caught that picture on my screen, it didn't even take a second thought to bring that phone up to me from the floor.

I couldn't hold the tears rolling down my eyes. I just turned the tap on and cried… A lot. After I finished crying, I came out of the washroom and went back to bed. But this time, I spent the rest of the night sobbing.

I don't know what to say… As much as I was buried in the weight of regrets of trusting someone and creating such a pathetic life for myself, I was even buried deeply by the weight of other regrets of having thoughts to end everything. And it was one of those kinds of moments when you don't have any idea how to deal with the situation. I was completely blank.

But, I told you there are very few decisions that I take very quick, like really quick. So, I bunk my classes the next day in the morning and headed towards the counselor on my campus. But before that, I had to do one thing… To check whether someone is noticing me going to the counseling cell.

Saying and doing are two different things. I decided to go to the counselor and that was much easier than actually going to the counselor. And I have to tell you that it was only possible because of my friend, Ashu's unwavering support throughout the process.

Man! It takes real bravery to go to the counseling cell because I was born in a place where mental health and everything related to it meant going insane. When you say, "I need to talk to a counselor," everyone will judge you. To be honest, that was the first time I approached it. And I wish I could have done that sooner.

I remember my first session with the specialist, as I entered her room, I was making sure no one finds me there because I was so scared of it, so scared of letting people know about my weaknesses.

Weaknesses! Just because I wasn't well mentally. Just because I was in tears, I thought I was the weakest person in the entire world. But as soon as I started talking with her, the specialist, my perspective on the whole thing changed completely. I remember walking into the cell, looking around to make sure no one was watching me, and when I got back to my hostel, I was like… I don't give a shit. I was up just after that one-hour session.

Oh, did I tell you that she was very sweet to offer me chocolate? But that time, I was not in the mood to even grab my favorite things. Yeah! Chocolate is my favorite. I love chocolates so much that I can literally treat myself to them.

In that one hour, we began with some fundamentals, such as an introduction. It was more of a friendly conversation than any kind of treatment. She was so friendly that I didn't even feel like I was meeting a counselor. I told her the entire story, everything I had thought about it, my flaws, my mistakes, everything. I was completely naked… I meant with my words in front of her.

And then, she told me, "Ekta, whatever happened to you was not your fault, your intentions were so genuine, but you can't control others. So, it's okay to not be okay. However, ending your life, or something, isn't a solution for anything. It can never ever be a solution. Rather than escaping from the problem, try to face it. Accept the challenge and fight. You took a step to talk about it here, it is itself the first step towards your success."

That's it! I needed that.

All I was doing was escape from the problem rather than face it. Why should I go away from it? I was true with my emotions. My feelings were genuine, and so was I.

That's all it took. I was instantly alright. All the heaviness that was there and I was buried inside it, seemed to be vanishing with just her simple words.

Some things are not just under our control. Let it be, the way it is. You can't force someone to stay in your life. The only thing you can do is, be happy living your life. Face every problem and try to fix it. You neither have control over your past nor future. You can neither go back nor move forward in time, all you can do is just enjoy the process, being in the present.

I wish I knew all these things a bit earlier in my life that nothing can hold your life. No matter what happens, your life goes on.

Just like your exams…

meeting with masterstrokes.

I was not a bright student. Well, I am still not the one. But, I have to say that I was born hard-working. I work really hard and that sometimes paid me off while other times, I had to suffer for that. Just like every coin has two sides.

My dad says, "Failures are the pillar of success." I say to him, "I could have made a beautiful house out of those pillars till now", with all those failures I had to face in my life.

The distance between your dream and your achievement is called struggle, the journey which decides whether you will reach your destination or not. But this journey is really greedy. It needs a lot of input in order to make you walk on its path to stay on it. It demands your patience, consistency, your time, your dedication, your hard work, your sweat, your blood, and everything else you can offer.

A lot... I know. But that's how it works. And it is tougher than it sounds, trust me! There is no shortcut to success. And like I said, no path is easy too. I wish I could discover something that would tell everyone their shortcut path to success.

I wish!

Well, I remember when I was in my school and if someone would ask me, "What is your aim?" My answer was really simple, "I wish to become a doctor."

Simple, easy, isn't it? Okay... I started my preparation during my intermediate studies. Before you say, I know that was really late when I was already struggling with my English.

Surprised?

I know, it's really strange, but I told you, I will be honest with you. And I won't be afraid to tell you that when I started preparing for my medical entrance test, I had two years to get the sheet in my parents' hands with the words Ekta Bera, AIR 1. Not kidding. Dreaming was really easier than pursuing that dream in reality.

In those two years, I was told to move from basics to advanced pieces of information. Well, when my classmates reached to advance, I struggled to grasp each line, and its meaning by searching in the Oxford dictionary.

That was offline time. Beautiful, but had its own drawbacks. Well, if I had exposure to the internet, my life would have been different. I actually can't say whether it would have been good or turned out to be worse but it would have been different for sure. And it was one of the things that I would wish to change if I get a chance.

I didn't realize that until the time my brother asked me, "Didi, suppose you have a superpower to go back in time, which time of your life would you wish to change, and why?" while we were walking to the market as we love to spend and have our best time walking around in the evening.

That day, I didn't answer him, I just made fun of him for asking me such a stupid question, but when I realized the depth of it and my life, I realized I would definitely want to change several things in my life including my childhood, to make it better. That's because…

When I was 14, and about to leave my first school, I wanted to get into another school. I wanted to get myself enrolled in a school of my choice but I wasn't that lucky to get the opportunity.

No offense. When I asked my family to get me enrolled in the best English medium school in town, I didn't get the right opportunity to meet my demand this time. Just because they were afraid I might get into more trouble after I get enrolled in an English medium school or maybe they might have to handle any insults because of me. And that's true! Because when all of their friends' children were in a good position, they were afraid to take me somewhere because I couldn't even greet somebody in English. I know that hurts, but that time it was even worse than it sounds. Man! I was literally lying on the negative side of the scale. And I was very casual about it until my family pointed a finger inside my eyes to make me realize that yes! I made the mistake of not learning English. When they asked for it while I was young, I continued to deny it.

Trust me! Until my intermediate studies, I didn't realize its importance. Well, that's because I didn't require it before. Oh did I tell you that my first school, I mean my primary education was all done in a Bengali medium School?

I studied in a Bengali medium school till class eight. And it was the only Bengali medium school in my town because I live in Jharkhand. Yeah! I know I could have enrolled in a Hindi or English medium at first. But, as you know my life is filled with surprises and it was one of a kind. I was young, so obviously, my parents enrolled me in a Bengali medium school in the hopes that I would retain our family culture. What they didn't realize was that by doing so, the academic scopes might be overlooked, and the scopes that I might come across in the future. That's how my primary education starts. No! I don't have any regrets about studying and knowing the Bengali language. It's just that I had no scope later on. If it would have been in a place where Bengali is valued much like West Bengal, I am sure, I would have had many opportunities to explore Bengali and get to do something out of it. But my hometown, however, is in Jharkhand. It is a state where studying alone is the most difficult part, and where can you expect to study a language of your choice and explore its scope? No way! It's not that simple.

My primary school was till class eight and there was no scope to study there after that. It means that I had to move to another school to continue my studies. It was the time when I was wondering about the best schools in the town to pursue my further schooling, I found the posh one among all in my city. I believed it would be great if I could study in that school but what I didn't realize was that to make up for that school, I needed to clear an English test. But by that time, I knew nothing about the language.

And that was the reason why my family was worried that I might get shame or maybe I would get hurt if I don't pass the test. But somehow the whole thing made me so upset that I cried the rest of the day. To be completely honest, I was a very stubborn child. I used to lock myself in a room without food whenever I was angry at something or someone. That's very childish of me, I know, but yeah! That was how I was. This could be because when you are the most loved and pampered child in your entire house, all your demands are met simply by saying them once, so I guess any child could turn out to be me, or maybe I am wrong. Maybe I'm just unsure what the exact reason for this is.

But you know what? When I'd lock myself inside the room

without food, after a while, one of my family members, or sometimes even the entire family would come to console me so that I'd forget everything and at least have my food. I suppose family is the most precious thing a person could ever have in his entire life.

And that day, nearly the same happened. I was locked in my room after hearing from my family and just cried… A lot. Then someone knocked on the door, I heard a few voices.

I believe, the people who love you, sometimes hurt you unintentionally. Because you can't hurt people whom you don't love.

I cried even louder and started sobbing too. I don't know why this happens all the time, whenever I cry or I'm angry, and if someone shows their concern, I cry even more, much louder than earlier.

But this time, I knew that was not because I was angry or something, I was trying to recollect their spoken words. Wasn't they right? What did I do for them till now? And of course, those questions from friends and neighbors would be making it even worse, "What does your daughter do?" "Where is she studying?" What percentage did she score in her class?"

I'm sure, these must be equally difficult for them too. I suppose I could have helped them at the time, or perhaps I couldn't… Because some things are beyond our control. Perhaps the most important reason was that I failed to recognize the opportunity knocking at my door. And when I did that, it left me with regrets later on.

I believe everyone in my family is an astrologer. They knew I would be requiring English at some point in my life, so they were tearing their epiglottis after me to learn it, but…

I just ignored them. And secondly, I believe English was not my cup of tea. Those sentence formation, tense, grammar, V1, V2, V3, V4, V5… No man! I was very bad at it.

I wish I could have understood their concerns a bit earlier in my life. But yes, I did squander the opportunity. And that was one of the reasons why my family didn't want to get me enrolled in the school of my choice. I wanted to study in an English medium school, and I didn't even know the "E" of English. That would have been terrible for both me and my family.

I just wish I could have heard my family telling me to learn English while they were hurting his epiglottis. But… Okay, as I previously stated, I couldn't go back in time. If it had been possible in any way, I would have changed one more thing about that time, the bond, my relationship with my family. That is something I deeply regret having.

I can't believe I had so much anger inside me for my own family that I couldn't attend the school of my choice. And just for that reason, I was growing a toxic relationship with my family.

Anyways, when I enrolled in another school, it happened to be a Hindi medium school in town. Although it was a Hindi medium school, I have to agree that my zeal to know English came from that School.

But wait… I wasn't successful at it yet.

It can't be easy for me. I was the kid whose paper had to be rechecked during the board exam. Yes, my batch was the most experimental of all time. We always had to put in extra effort to get everything to work out. During our 10th All of our papers were rechecked on our 10th board exam. To make it even more experimental, I decided to go to

Vishakhapatnam for my intermediate studies. I still don't know how to react to that... I will tell you why.

First, Visakhapatnam is a city in South India, and it is one of the Telugu-speaking cities. So, one thing I was sure about was that this was going to be tough. And second... You guessed that, right? My relationship with English, which I was very good at!

As much as it was tough, unexpected too.

When I planned to go there, I thought it would be very easy and once I go there, I will be featured in newspapers. My parents would get interviewed by news reporters, there will be photoshoots all around, and everyone will ask me for tips and tricks to crack the medical entrance exam in one go because I was able to make it to AIR 1.

Man! I can't tell you how high my expectations had risen. My foot was not on the ground because I was daydreaming about my results. But you know what, when you skip reality, you go higher and higher, and when you realize all the facts and look down, there will be no ground to stand on.

I had so many fantasies about my future that when I looked down... There were no grounds, as I said. When we moved to the second year of our intermediate studies and everyone else was focusing on that, I was still stuck, struggling to understand my first yearbooks. When we are asked to concentrate on the weightage of those two years in the entrance exam, we discover that the first year accounts for 60% and the second 40%.

Hats off to my self-assurance. Until that point, whenever my family asked how I was doing with my preparation, I would respond with the same assurance that I had when I started these two years of study.

I maintained that same level of assurance until my results were out. And then I realized I couldn't do it. For me, the entrance was out of the box.

I was lying to my family, telling them that I was working hard, that I would do the best of my capabilities, and that I would make them proud. But… I was late for all of them. When I had to focus on my present, I was still trying to figure out everything about my past and about myself.

I never thought that just a single ignorance could turn my life entirely into a different one. English… Not just my failure, but my struggle to make it up to my failure was even more traumatic than it may sound.

Wait… Did I tell you that this was the first time I was moving away from my home, from my family, and from everything in my comfort zone? But yes, confidence was everything that I was wearing all my way to it. I thought, there is no one better than me. But man! I was the queen of frogs in that well. I didn't realize what the outer world would seem like. I thought there would be greetings, and people would be waiting for me there where I would walk, and they would lay rose petals all over the road for me. Nothing like that… Not at all!

When I entered my room, there was more silence than it was on my parent's faces that I had ever seen. When I reached up to the door and opened it, there were already two girls inside the room. I guess they reached one or two days earlier than me.

I was standing with my bags facing my room, the two girls over there looked me up and down. As if they were not expecting someone like that. I said, "Hi", then there was a pause of ten seconds from both sides, and "Hi…", one of them said to me, with no excitement. I didn't understand what was in there and entered inside, placed my bags, and went to the washroom to freshen up.

As I did, I could hear giggling sounds from my room. It was them. The two of them were talking about me! Well, was I that important to them?

Not at all!

I heard one of them saying, "Did you see her clothes? And her look?" I know, I didn't tell you, I was not at all good-looking, well, I am still not the one. And my skin color, yeah! On the darker side, they talked about that too. I already knew I am not any beautiful model but definitely I didn't deserve their words. The more I tried to listen to them, the more I was hurt.

I didn't know how to react because I'd never seen anything like it before in my life. But, isn't there a first time for everything? It was the first time I had been away from my family and home. So I didn't want to bother them by talking about my roommates. But it was becoming increasingly difficult to stay with them every day. Every day, they would make fun of me in some way. They somehow became aware of all of my weaknesses, which was my greatest fear when I met them.

I was afraid that they would bury my slits inside the salts. And speak of the fears... It just happened! Every day, every time, every moment, I was getting more and more suffocated. It was tougher than I had thought it would be. Well, thankfully, there was something called homesickness, it was a ten days holiday for every new joinee. Aah! Still better. I was relieved that I could at least get ten days away from them.

The ten-day period flew by. It didn't feel like a holiday at all. And then it's time to head back to the hostel. I was worried about having to face them again. So, on my way home, and back to the hostel, I made a decision. I figured I'd tell my warden and ask her if she could move me to a different room. And the very first thing I did after my father dropped me off at the hostel was to report to the warden about everything, from the beginning to the end. Furthermore, I requested that she move me to another room because I couldn't even breathe in that one.

My warden was very kind to assist me. I relocated to a room right next to my previous one. Obviously, the rooms were not soundproof! So they used to yell from their room now and then, but I had a mantra… Ignore them. My new roommates were all friendly and helpful. Finally, with their help, I was able to easily complete my two-year stay in the hostel. But somewhere in there, I was still struggling with my academics.

Not only me but my family saw its huge reflection on my result day. And then… What?

My life changed its route!

aimless aim

Talking about routes…

Since my childhood, I was taught about goals that are not very different yet… Finish studies at 24, get a stable job, and get married by 26. This is the aim, this is what successful life should look like.

For me going out is getting difficult nowadays as everyone asks "When are you getting married?" I wonder why they are more concerned about my marriage than my own family? My family never asks me for marriage.

I don't understand why getting married is so important in our society, especially when you are a female. Well, I believe if others should be concerned about something then it should be health and career, not outside that.

Just the last time when I was working on my thesis proposal for my Ph.D. my parents came inside my room. Well, when both of your parents come to your room together, it means there is something like "We need to talk."

My adrenaline went up to its peak… I knew it was one of those awaited moments to discuss a career. But it wasn't.

I was surprised that my parents said, "Beta, in our society, people your age get married but we know you have outstanding career plans and you are not thinking about your marriage right now. We understand that it might be getting difficult for you to get outside, people might ask you about your marriage plans and suddenly you might be feeling all the pressure in your head." I shut my laptop down and stared at them and didn't say any words because I wanted to listen to them more and more. They added, "We just want you to know that we are here to support you with your every decision. We are here to follow you with your dreams. We are here to assure you that no matter what people think or say about you, we will always be there with you."

I don't know what to say and what should I feel? I was surprised, happy and the proudest that I have had them.

I know, it might be getting difficult for them too when people would be asking about their daughter's marriage plans. I know they might be getting hurt when people would say things like, "Have you saved dowry for your daughter's marriage?" "If you don't get your daughter married then she will be having problems during her pregnancy."

I don't know how they must be handling such things. But I knew one thing… I am the luckiest daughter.

Well, I believe time has the superpower to change anything and everything. When I was young I saw my family as a bit traditional in the sense that they didn't understand anything outside academia.

I saw some of my friends painting really well and getting prizes for their paintings. I was a kid and that fascinated me in a way that I asked my family to get me enrolled in a painting class, they said it was not my time to learn something outside academia. Well, that's fine, I understand. But it was me who loved to learn, who was passionate about learning and trying new things and I genuinely wanted to learn painting but…

Do you know what Adwika, we people, learn mostly from

our environment and especially when you are a kid? Because you don't know the difference between right or wrong for you when you are at a younger age. You believe that whatever you think for yourself is the only right choice for you. And when things don't happen according to you, it's when you get upset about it. It feels as if your dream was broken.

Well, okay! I am a good girl. I always listen to my family. So, why not this time? I tried to forget about painting. It took a bit of time. Because obviously, it is tough to get back to reality when you have already fantasized about one particular thing so much.

And after a few days, something surprising happened. My family who didn't agree to get me enrolled in painting class, now want me to learn music.

Ahh! I told you time can change everything.

Well, I think I didn't tell you a secret? I love music as much as I love eating chicken. Sometimes you do things unknowingly but it turns out to be the best, just like my music.

It all started when I didn't even know that something called music even exists when my family enrolled me in a music class and now I have to agree it is the best thing that ever happened in my life. Isn't it weird how you fall for something that you weren't even aware of a few times back? My love for music has taken a shape like that.

I still remember asking them, "Where are we going?" when we were on our way to my admission there. I had absolutely no idea what was going to happen there. "To your music class," my mother said.

What's that, a music class? What? How? I mean… Why? My mind was still processing what had happened.

Nonetheless, I asked her, "Why am I going to a music class?" "Because I wanted to learn music but couldn't, so I want you to fulfill my dream," my mother explained. That doesn't make sense now, but it was very emotional for me at the time. Just like any melodrama in a Bollywood film.

Just kidding! It was actually emotional for me. I decided I will learn music. Well, as if I was given any other choice.

Finally, we reached there… Yes! I am still talking about my music class. All the paperwork was done and I was told to attend twice a week which will be on Saturdays and Sundays. Okay! That's okay! I will come.

Trust me, I attended that class for just one month and I was already in love with it. I developed a very keen interest in music. I know, music has the magic to make you fall for it. And the more I attended classes, the more I could see my interest growing in music. It was just like a match made in heaven.

But then I was about to leave my hometown for intermediate studies. Remember, I told you, it was the first time I was going away from everything, including music. Well, it felt like I just had a break-up with my music.

This time my circumstances were not in my favor so that I could pursue music for the rest of my life because I knew it was not a favorable time for me to learn anything outside academia.

This break-up was a bit brutal. As I told you about fantasizing dreams. Well, I already imagined myself as a singer. But…

Again the route changed.

This time, I knew the time didn't come for me to learn anything else outside my academics, so, I left everything out there, and focused on only one direction. As they say,

"All play and no work makes Jack a mere toy." I started with my academic journey.

Times were very different at that moment. It was a time when there was a stereotype built around career choices. Do you know, Adwika? At that time the career choice was gender-specific. It was believed that if it was a boy then he would be an engineer and if it was a girl then she would be a doctor. And the problem with these things is nothing but pressure. The abundant pressure that society puts inside a kid's head is just outside someone's imagination.

Being a girl, it was an immense pressure for me to become a doctor, and I was even convinced because all of my friends had already set their aim to become a doctor. And I believe it was that moment when I made another mistake.

A mistake that I didn't pursue because I wanted to. It was because everyone does that. It was the time when I failed the medical entrance exam plus I scored fewer marks on my boards. Well, it's less than my 10th board.

And didn't I already mention to you that in my intermediate studies, I have seen the worst and the best? The friendship I did, turned out to be a betrayal… I didn't get a chance in the medical entrance exam… But yet something best happened.

My English has improved. At least I could understand what was written in each line of the book, and I don't even have to carry an Oxford dictionary along with me the whole time.

After my boards, I appeared for medical entrance exams with several other exams so that at least I got to know about it. As everyone says, "More tests you appear to mean more experience you are getting about your destination test." But I must tell you it doesn't work like that. It is more of trying luck than experience gaining.

After the results were out, obviously, I couldn't pass the medical entrance exam but I cleared the JCECE Agriculture exam with a rank of 121. But my habit of fantasizing about dreams… The only reason that made me take a chance on myself. As I already had imagined myself as a Neurologist, and not just the Neurologist but the best one in my country. So, I decided to invest one more year of my life.

I tried again next year. And just like the previous year, I couldn't make it to the medical entrance exam. And the funny thing is, I don't even remember what rank I received because I couldn't remember the eight-digit number. However, I managed to hold a rank of 136 in the JCECE Agriculture exam. I was called for the counseling from the JCECE end, but I thought it would be better not to attend that.

Now… What? I knew I had another turn to take on my way. From Ekta to a zoologist, my journey was just about to begin.

I was eighteen years old at the time. I couldn't afford to lose another year of my life, so I needed to enroll in college. Because I knew deep down that I couldn't do it. This medical entrance was impassable to me. It took a while for that to sink in, but I did it in the end. I took a step toward a new journey after releasing all of the weight of my dreams from my shoulders.

I should be disappointed that I was unable to realize my ambitions, that I was unable to fulfill both my own and my family's dreams. I couldn't make them proud. I should be disappointed that I was already a failure. But… I was overjoyed. I was relieved to know that a brand new chapter was about to begin. All I had to do was turn the page. Yes, I did! And it made it even easier because I love zoology, I genuinely do!

I didn't think much about it. I was prepared for the worst and headed toward the new journey that was just about to begin. I knew, my life can't get any worse than this. And I was right. As I entered my hostel, I found eight of them just like me. They look too innocent to make fun of me.

When I started talking to each one of them, I came to know they all are from the same state. I inhaled and then exhaled a deep breath of relief. Adwika, do you understand what that means? That means I don't have to worry about being judged for my clothes, my fashion sense, whether I'm rich or poor, whether I can speak English, or anything else. Among them, one of them was in my class, and the rest were juniors. That means I could rag them and let all my frustrations out, so much anger from my previous hostel, so much I had learned… But I didn't. I never thought of treating them the way I was being treated in my previous hostel. I was really friendly, and I guess, I was changing bit by bit after I met them. Changing in a good sense. I don't know why I am like this, but yes! I can't treat people the way they deserve. Okay! Not all but some of them do.

I had no idea Ranchi would be the source of so many wonderful memories in my life. I found many, and I lost many, but the process continued… Learning. My actual learning began there, I must say. I no longer had to sift through the dictionary to figure out what a line in my textbook meant.

Everything was going so smoothly. But remember, I told you life can't be smooth all the time. It has to get rough sometimes to get even smoother next time.

Exams again… This time, selection tests were announced, which would most likely take place before the first year's final exams. And it was serious, but not to be taken seriously. Wait a minute, let me rephrase that. Selection tests were held to determine whether or not a student would be able to compete in the final round. However, its grades will not be added to your grade sheet.

I happened to be the most interactive in my entire class. Further, it was obvious that all the teachers would expect more from me. And more than that, I was so confident that, ahh! I will just rock the papers. I was so prepared for it. And so it went. But when the results were announced, oh wait… They were not announced, they were shown in front of the whole classroom. That means, everyone will get to know each other's marks and can judge too. When I was called by name, everyone gave me a look like "Obviously! She would score good marks." And the next moment, I couldn't believe my own eyes. I failed by two marks. The building, yeah! My confidence was falling down because of an earthquake. I came down to earth again. And they all were laughing behind me. I heard them saying, "She was a talented and most interactive girl, how could… ?"

Trust me, this "how?" raises more problems than the actual problem. What will people think about me? How will my parents react to this? How would I even face my roommates? How is this… How is that… How… How, and how… It doesn't end. At that time, I thought more about those "how?" than I had ever thought about my marks.

What next?

I was not alone in holding that off from my scores. There were about twenty people who were holding almost the same sheet. That means, there were the rest fifteen who could pass. That felt a bit better. At least I was not the only one in this. Then, we all were asked to appear for the test again with a condition, this time we all had to pass.

Remember I told you who was in my class? That was my roommate. Yes, she received passing grades. So I took her paper and mine, and this time I did the most daring thing I'd ever done in my life. I compared the two. Yes, I did it. But not to judge her paper or her, but to compare what made these two different. Because she was the one I taught the concepts to several times. I noticed a significant difference between comprehending a concept and writing about it. I could easily understand all of the concepts, but when it came to writing about them… I lacked that skill.

It was time to work on my skills. I started learning from her about writing. I observed how she writes and then worked on mine. In that one week before our re-test, I was all set with my writing. I appeared for the test and scored good marks this time. Not full marks, but not fail, definitely. I couldn't see this happening in my final exams. I needed to work more this time. I started working on my writing more and more and more until I made sixty-nine percent in my first-year finals. Not great, I know! But certainly, not bad.

By that time, I improved my understanding of concepts, basics, and writing. And I was consistently improving with my marks too. Everything was running smoothly. But you know my life, right?

Well, I forgot to tell you one thing I did the one really daring task all the time. While I was in Ranchi, my roommates decided to read newspapers daily because we felt out of this world and we needed to know at least something about daily news, and what is happening outside our room.

And you know what? The newspapers of those days were more about which rickshaw puller's kid could clear the UPSC exam or which fruit vendor's son had topped the UPSC at one attempt. I have to agree that newspapers did a really great job putting the bold catchy headlines about UPSC and its results.

I know UPSC is considered to be one of the toughest exams in our country and getting it cleared at one go is something that catches everyone's eye, at least it did mine. I was so fascinated that I thought I could give it a try. I didn't realize that a try is not enough, UPSC demands everything. The abundant knowledge, the consistent patience, dedication, and the most of your hard work.

Well, you don't have to be an expert in any subject but UPSC demands knowledge of every subject. And except for science, I was really dumb at all other subjects. Oh, did I tell you my marks which I scored in social science in my class 10th, 47 including practical marks? Harsh to digest. But it is a brutal truth, the truth of my social science knowledge.

And still, another truth was that I decided to prepare for it. But as I did, I didn't fail this time, I left it midway.

And I think that is even worse than failing. But how can you expect the result out of something when you don't even plan properly to execute it? I agree I made a mistake in approaching it. But okay! I couldn't help it.

After I graduated from college, I knew I couldn't do a 9-5 job sitting in front of the screen, so that means I was left with one door.

It was written all over it that my next chapter holds M.Sc. Trust me, as soon as I was in, I wondered isn't it something that I always wanted to do? It was the time when I realized that yes! Now all my dots are getting connected.

When I came back, I did have a good grade. I had an M.Sc. degree in my hands but one thing I didn't have was clarity. I was unclear about my achievement, my growth, and my success. I was unhappy. I knew I was educated but I didn't know my worth. I didn't know whether I had achieved anything till then.

That's it!

It's time, not to waste time. Now, it's time to focus on things that I couldn't do and the things that I think I can't do. It's time to end something to find something new, something better.

Delete Created with Sketch.

52

II. acuity in vision.

changes.

It's always better to find another direction when the road you are traveling has huge traffic. It's always better not to waste time on things that we can't control, the things that hold us back.

It's better to work for the better!

Two years…

I took a break of two years, to work on myself, and to find answers to some questions. This time, no What-ifs, rather What next? What better can I do? What more can I do? And what else can I do?

Trust me, some breaks are just worth taking. Not for anyone else, but for you. Because running after things to please the World has nothing to do with one's life except losing self. I can't make something better which I don't like to do at all. So, why just not identify things that I can work through and get better? It's time, not to focus on the World, but on self. It's time to be myself.

The last two years have completely overshadowed the previous twenty-three years of my life, in which I was living with regrets. I persevered in the face of adversity. But, most importantly, I enjoyed discovering new ways to improve myself and opening new doors when one was closed.

I enjoyed being myself.

That was exactly what I needed. Because I needed to determine my own level of success. It was time for me to start living my own life. When I was regretting why I had failed in the first place, I needed to focus on the other 1000 ways to make things better which my own failures had taught me.

Starting something, and failing, is just another way to make things better for the next time.

The greatest of all, in those two years, I have learned many things, many great lessons. And now, there is no going back… Not at all!

I believe I was already successful when I was able to define my own success!

another side of the coin.

Every coin has two sides.

That's true! And both sides can't be viewed standing at one point. When we have night, the other half of the world has a day, doesn't it?
Every darkest night is followed by a bright morning. Just like, you can't succeed if you don't fail. And that is the reason I believe, failures are the most important part of our lives.
Our failures leave scars on one side but on another, teach us the greatest lessons. Greatest of all, to find another way to make things even better than before, better for next time, and follow.
Our lives are not worth trying to forget our failures. It's meant to learn from them, and define another way of success.
All I needed was to embrace my failures, learn from them and re-start my journey. The journey of exploration, the journey to find me. And the journey to make things better.
I did. I embrace everything, which I have, and which I don't. No regrets!
Because now, the only focus was to find… What can I have?

chasing goals, not dreams.

Your dreams come true… When you achieve your goal.

To make your dream a reality, I believe the first step is to set a goal, or set of goals, and begin chasing them. Running after goals, whether short-term or long-term, is important because there are several steps involved in a journey, and you will be able to achieve all of them only after you have succeeded in the first. Dreams can be unrealistic at times because there are no boundaries to them. It is the reality that brings you down to earth, it is a goal that makes you realize what is and is not achievable.
A goal should be:

G:Genuine
O:Optimistic
A:Achievable
L:Learning

I made the mistake of chasing my dream when I needed to chase my goals. I set some very unrealistic goals for myself. Even though I tried a lot, deep inside, I knew it would be very tough for me and so, the possibility of failing was also there. In fact, the percentage of achieving that was tougher than failing.
I was not even unaware of English, I couldn't even understand what had been written in my textbooks when I

dreamt of becoming a doctor. How can it be achieved? The world never stops for anything or anyone. It's you who has to catch up with the speed of it.

Definitely, I was lost. My dream was broken. And I failed.

Again, when I had just begun to improve my English comprehension, I fantasized about becoming an IAS officer, which seemed far-fetched to me. Again, I was just an enthusiast about my dream; I was so enthralled by it that I forgot that a UPSC requires all of the fundamentals, especially social science, which I was clearly not good at.

I knew again that it would be very tough for me, but still, my excitement took me to take a step toward it and I started its preparation.

But then what next? I failed again.

All these dreams and failures have taught me one thing: a destination is always followed by several stops. And I can never reach the top of the mountain if I don't focus on one small detail at a time.

working for worth.

Definitely, education gives knowledge. But the right ability and assurance that you can use your existing knowledge are defined by skills. Education and skills are just like matches made in heaven.

Well, education can be taught, but skills require learning, a genuine interest, hard work, and a lot of practice for it.

I could call myself educated when I graduated from university. I also had an A-Grade master's degree. But when it came to putting the knowledge to use, I fell short.

I've never worked hard to improve my skills. Nobody told me I needed to work on them, and I had no desire to learn anything about them. I was mistaken in believing that I would never need any skill because it was instilled in me. No way! Skills can be inherited as well as acquired. Well, yeah! A skill may necessitate both inborn talent and practice.

After getting multiple rejections from companies that I applied for jobs, I didn't quit this time. Instead, I decided to work, work for better and for worse. I decided to get through this.

Self-development.

I added a new term self-development to my life's dictionary and started working on it one by one.

reading.

This is the first skill I worked on. Frankly, I had never even thought of reading anything outside my academia. But when it came to working for self-development, the least I could do was read.

From zero to now a hundreds of books including non-fiction, fiction, online and paper-back, I have maintained a library.

I must say, not just in vocabulary, but also in understanding, thought processes, talking skills, sentence framing, and abundance of knowledge… Reading has given me everything.

writing.

Although, I enjoyed writing but never thought I would be loving this one day. Yes! My love for writing developed very recently but within no time, I started falling for it, because this is so magical.

For expression, we all need a medium. And I don't think there is any better medium than writing for self-expression. Writing itself is a creative field, so, there is always room for development, it can never get old.

It may sound weird but it's true, I find writing as a friend who doesn't judge me while I express myself, with all of my naked truths.

Writing on its own is beautiful, but as a writer, you become an even more beautiful person inside out.

It didn't require me to have a professional degree in order to be a writer. I just started with it, and with practice and my love for writing, I could make it up till now.

Not just in developing content but in the development of a

better person, writing has helped me in many ways such as controlling emotions, better self-expression, better speaking abilities, better interaction with people, and a lot of other things too.

thinking ability & openness.

I know, I was open-minded since I was exposed to several outside things, cultures, and people. I learned to observe everything in my surroundings. But only observance was not enough, I couldn't develop a thought instantly.

But it has evolved over time, and I must say that it has grown more since I began working on my writing skills. Now I can think about something and form an opinion about it. I began to gain a better understanding of the other person's point of view.

Earlier, there was "Me" in everything, which created a huge communication gap between me and other people around me. But now this is not anymore! There is "We" when I am talking to someone or in front of others. I listen to them, analyze the situation and then come to a decision.

I have noticed that this has helped me control my anger issues. I used to get very irritated with even smaller things when something doesn't happen just like I wanted it to be. I realized this was a bigger problem because I didn't understand what the other person must be going through, what the circumstances were, and whether it was viable or not. Well, I have worked through this. Now, I understand in a multi-directional way and come to a better solution. It helped me to make decisions better and more effectively.

designing.

I used to draw since childhood. I even had an interest in sketching. Well, if not then, why not now? At that time, I didn't have a scope to pursue my interest but now it would be very unfair if I don't make my old interest alive when I have all the facilities.

Now, however, the time has changed. It's all digital. I thought it would be useful for my technical skills as well, so I began designing digitally and am now a self-taught UX-UI designer. I've worked on several startup design interfaces, which I believe will go live very soon, and I've also designed for the fashion industry, precisely merchandise.

I had never thought that my childhood interest would work so well for me. But, yeah! It did.

And I really enjoy designing.

web development.

Now the next part, when you have a design with you, is to develop that design and make it interactive, that's when user experience comes in.

I didn't have any prior knowledge in this field, and none in my family encouraged this ever. It came in after I started designing. Isn't that beautiful? You start with one, and then go to the next, then next and next and there is no absolute finish line to it.

It all happened so. I researched a bit about this and came to know, what better I could do? Web development.

Starting with web development would be easy. So, I headed over to the online course available and started learning it. Now, I can call myself a full-stack web developer. I have developed more than ten complete interactive websites.

And most importantly, I enjoy doing this.

I started with one, and everything else just happens like that. I must say, even if skills don't get someone placed in a unicorn company with a huge salary bracket, it doesn't leave a person empty-handed. With every skill, the person gets better and better and better.

starting over again.

Learning is like a deep sea, the more you go deeper, the more you get to grab it.

But to dive into the sea, first, you need to reach it.

While growing up, we all develop some interests but they remain as interests only, and we fail to pursue that. I understand that starting itself is a tougher task than actually doing it.

I always blamed my past that I was unable to pursue my interests. Well, instead of blaming my past, if I would have started it right away, wouldn't that make better sense? Yes! It would.

I tell you, blaming the past is easier, but wasting time blaming the whole past… Doesn't that mean I am making the same mistake again?

What if I had developed an interest in painting while I was young? So why didn't my family allow me to pursue my interest? So what if I didn't get enrolled in the school of my choice? So what if I stay in the hostel, I can't work on my health?

If my conditions didn't allow me to pursue my interest while I was a child, I can still pursue that. If my parents didn't get me enrolled in the school of my choice because I could learn better, I can still learn better. Even if I am staying in the hostel, I still can avoid junk food outside, I still can take out 30 minutes of time for exercise if not 1 hour. I could do it, but the problem was I didn't want to do it because it was easier than starting something. I literally wasted more time overthinking the circumstances which might have been better in the past.

Twenty-three years of my life, I just wasted my time making excuses. But, not anymore… During these two years, I knew that if I have to do something, I need to start working on it today. Be it my health goals or self-development, or be it pursuing any interest… All I needed was to get started. I did and I succeeded.

All it required was one genuine interest and the first courage to start, rest everything will fall into its place. I have understood that there is no scope for starting anything tomorrow. It should always be today.

Because now is the time!

holding consistency.

Every coin has two sides, definitely! Success and failures are the two sides of a journey. But one can only reach the destination, if he stays in it, stays till the very last moment.

And like so every goal needs consistency. Consistent efforts, consistent dedication, consistent hard work, and consistent focus… A goal requires everything.

If I think, I would dream of something and just by working two days in a row, I will make it come true. No way! It doesn't work like a semester paper which I know, most of us study the day before the actual exam. That is our savior, not a dream comes true.

Life goals are not saviors, these are meant to be chased, chased to make a dream come true. It demands every day, every moment, every bit of hard work. And in fact, each time, a bit more effort. It requires those extra miles to walk. It tests how far you can even travel for it so that you are paid for it accordingly.

Be it UPSC or medical entrance test, or any goal, everything requires consistent hard work for it. Well, I failed in the first place because I was not consistent, I was impatient. Or maybe, I wasn't ready yet to put in my consistent effort.

But now, I have learned. I have learned to be more patient, to be consistent, and work hard. Well, yeah! I still don't consider myself successful yet, but still I am successful because I am working towards it, every day, every time, and every moment. In fact, each time with more and more extra effort.

practical with backup.

Emergency exit!

Every place has an emergency exit. Isn't it? That's very practical thinking because the future is really uncertain. Anything can happen, so, better to keep everything safe, and prepare for the worst.

Doesn't that exactly go with our lives? It is uncertain too. We don't have any idea what is going to happen in the future. The dream that we see now, might not come true in the future. We might want to go somewhere but be taken to somewhere else. Anything, literally, anything can happen.

In such a case, it would be easier when we have plans, rather than a single plan. Love for dreams is good but the practicality of achieving them is real.

Well, yeah! Emergency exits are meant for safekeeping, used only in case of a real emergency scenario. Likewise, there is no harm in having a backup plan for life, just in case, everything goes wrong. Yes! Only when everything goes wrong.

Because, when you have a visible exit in front of you, why would you make an extra effort to find the emergency window and move out? Doesn't make any sense, right?

I was mistaken. I was always told that the aim should be one, and with all my dedication and efforts, I can achieve that definitely. I wish someone would have told me that life runs with all the probabilities. Yes! That probability which we generally skip in our classes, and teachers also don't stress that too much. Because everyone believes that probability is a game for children, everyone knows it already.

But... When you start studying that, you go deeper and deeper, and deeper. There is no end to it. There are some facts that only studying can get us to know about. There are some complexities that only our teachers can solve. And then when you appear for the tests, you get lesser marks, sometimes don't even pass, because most of the questions come from the chapters that you left.

I wish someone had told me that there is a probability, which means that there is an equal chance of success and failure. If there is a 50 percent chance of success, a 50 percent is still reserved for failure. Only consistent efforts will result in a perfect score. However, if everything goes wrong, the only thing that can save your life is an escape plan or a re-test. Probability, right?

Then it's just a matter of being practical.

Being successful with a backup plan is much better than dying unsuccessful.

learning the art.

Time management...

This was something I couldn't find myself a fit for. I didn't know what to prioritize and what not? But in those two years, I have learned many things including prioritizing too.

Everything is important in life, be it family, career, friendship, love, health, or any other things. So, I divide my day into small sections so that I can manage my time very well.

The harshest truth is that there are only 24 hours a day. And everyone has the same 24 hours time. Some are utilizing their time, while some are absolutely wasting it. It's upon you, whether you want to well-utilize time or simply waste it.

Well, I was the second kind of person. I used to waste most of my time, doing literally nothing. And all thanks to social media which event helped me waste more of my time. I kept on making excuses that I don't have time for other things, which could make my life a bit better at an earlier stage.

Now that I understand the importance of everything, I offer the least and the most precious thing that I can, my time.

I am a writer, a designer, a developer, and a zoologist. I love them so much that I can't leave any of them, and most importantly do I even want to leave any of them?

The answer is No!
That's why I make time for every skill, to brush them up, because, doesn't practice make a man perfect?
Well, apart from that, health is also important which requires healthy habits like sound sleep, a good diet, regular exercise, and meditation. And then the grooming, yes! I believe I deserve grooming. So, for me, I take care of my skin, dressing, and all other things.
Then above all, my family. I make sure I can offer them my time as much as possible. And for that, they don't have to ask me. It is my responsibility to spend time with them.
Oh, yes! I do go out. I make time for things which I like, such as listening to music, roaming around, shopping, and all other things.
I know that doing a lot of things requires a lot of time and energy. But trust me, if it is well-planned, and executed efficiently, one can do everything… Literally everything.
Everyone does have twenty-four hours but not everyone's twenty-four hours are the same.

Because time is relative… For everyone.

discarding parasites.

All the distractions…

I know, it is an era of the internet, which means more pieces of information. But the more we try to gather information, the more we get distracted.

There are several distractions but I believe, social media has topped the list when it comes to distractions, at least for me. I used to spend more time on absolutely unnecessary things than investing my time on something that could give me some returns.

I didn't realize it, but slowly, I was addicted to it.

As soon as I decided to work on myself, the first thing that came into my mind was time management, and for that, the deadly parasite was my social media. It was tough at first but I could identify my distractions and that helped me to get rid of them.

I decided to remove all my distractions from my life. I deleted all my social media accounts and set timers on apps that were actually consuming my time so that I could focus more on important things.

And I am more than happy that I did that. Because I did it for myself, to make my life better.

understanding the wealth.

I haven't come across anything more common than this line "Health is Wealth". And I am sure everyone has come across this some or the other time in their lives. But the problem is, how many do actually understand this?

It is simple yet has a deeper meaning than lying to it. I don't know why we don't even take our health into consideration. We keep ourselves busy with our careers and other kinds of stuff so much that we forget to take care of our most important thing, our health. Our health is something that needs our care, and in return, it pays off too. I think that's why this line is more common than anyone can think of.

We always search for a cure when it barely costs us for its prevention. No offense, if something has grasped us, we will look for its cure, obviously! But what is the guarantee that it won't come back to you again? But if we take care of our health in the first place, does it have any scope to come? I believe no! After all, "Prevention is way better than cure." Isn't it so?

Just two years back, I was literally a couch potato. That's probably because of two reasons, I had no time to take care of my health, and the second, I was making excuses when I actually needed to take action.

I had my menarche when I was in ninth grade, and I was later diagnosed with PCOS. People with PCOS can only understand the pain of periods after a huge time gap between cycles, and other physiological changes in the body can make a person worse than ever. The number of mood swings and kilos of medications they are taking is not worth it. And especially when you consider that you will have to accept everything as it is for the rest of your life. Yes! My doctor had told me that there was no way to cure this.

That I accepted. I accepted the fact that I would have to live with a condition for which there is no cure. Anyway, by taking those medications, I was making room in my body for other health issues. When I returned home and spoke with a doctor, she advised me to undergo multiple tests.

I didn't have a choice at the time because I hadn't been able to concentrate on my studies or anything else for more than six months. Vomiting and headaches were becoming more severe by the day. Then there was the time when I couldn't even walk for 5 minutes.

I didn't know what I was going through until my test reports came out with the Classical form of PCOS, Migraine, the lowest vitamin D, and Thyroid.

For the time being, I reasoned that it would have been preferable if I had died of cancer. This could be the end of my life all at once, and it's far better than dying slowly every day.

I didn't have any idea what to do, which medicine to take first, which one to tackle first. And that's when I realized, man! I am a zoologist and research is my field. I did! I researched everything about each one of my health problems and found a common string in between all of them. It's the lifestyle.

I can understand this was a gift that I acquired from my hostel life which cost me my health. Loads of junk, late-night awakenings, wasting time on Facebook, no proper rest, and then making excuses to take out time for a workout. I had absolutely not even zero, a negative movement. I weighed myself at 80 kgs when I came back home, something I had realized earlier when none of my clothes were getting fit into me. I knew I had to work on my health, but… I told you, I was so lazy to start.

Now that I've been diagnosed with a worst-case scenario for my health and told I'd have to take medications for the rest of my life, I figured, hey, I'm already a lab rat because I've been experimented on for the last 1two years with various medicines to treat my PCOS, so why not take a chance myself? I wasn't sure whether to start it or not, but one thing was certain: I couldn't live with those medications for the rest of my life. Because your physical health causes more than just physical problems, it also affects your mental health, which is even worse, as I have already experienced once in my life and I didn't want that to happen again to me.

I started!

I believe, the moment I started with a first step is the moment I succeeded one step ahead of my way.

I basically focused on three main things:

sleep.

When I was in the hostel, I could barely sleep for 4-5 hours a night, so, I thought it would be much better to start with my sleep. At first, I did have trouble sleeping, but after one week, I started noticing the results.

Now, I sleep for 7-8 hours a night. This not only helped

me slow down my migraine but also, helped me stay a bit calm, unlike earlier times when my lesser sleep caused me to have an irritating mood the whole day.

I was a complete night owl, but now I go to bed by 9:30 P.M. at night, spend 30 minutes with my cellphone, watch some videos and then sleep by 10:00 or 10:30 P.M. sometimes and then wake up between 5:30 to 6:30 A.M. Because I believe everything starts with great sleep.

exercise and meditation.

Ahh! This was something I struggled with a lot. As I already told you, I was a couch potato, literally a negative movement. For me, I could go to the washroom from my bed, that was the biggest task of the day.

When I started with exercise, I used to spend 30 minutes a day, and then I increased it slowly. I still remember when I started, I started with walking, then brisk walking, and then running with a mix of some stretching.

Every other day, I felt like quitting everything. But after one month when I saw the results on my weighing scale, I was shocked. I lost 5 kg. I was so excited and motivated that I decided to work even harder. But the next month was down. I didn't get a result, instead, I gained 2kg of the weight I had lost.

I was so frustrated again, but this time I thought I could do better. I consulted a dietician and she asked me to follow all her instructions. She guided me throughout the process. She used to provide me with a diet for a week. And honestly, my journey was not at all easy. I saw many ups and downs but after eight months of hard work, I made it.

I lost 22kg. I ran two 5K within 30 minutes. It's been almost two years now, and I haven't regained any extra weight back, which I think is the toughest task when you start your weight loss journey.

Because one thing I was very clear that I am doing it for myself. This is not anything that I need to lose a certain weight and then when I reach my target, I can quit it. No! I was clear that this is going to be forever. This is not a weight loss journey, this is a journey to stay healthy, the journey of a complete lifestyle change, for the better.

Not just weight loss, but I have realized when I exercise, I feel really happy and that is the reason I don't fail to take out one hour for myself to stay happy for the rest of the day and absolutely have no struggle falling asleep.

As far as meditation is concerned, I spend just ten minutes a day. When I came across the research that its magic is not something new or unknown to anyone, I decided to spend just ten minutes. Trust me, it has improved my focus, and my moods, and I believe it helped me in my creativity, basically in the thinking process. When you are getting many benefits just for spending ten minutes, then why not? These ten minutes are worth spending for me. It's been two years now, and I am practising meditation. I still didn't get anything to prove my learning to date, but yes! As soon as I get it, I would definitely love to dig its roots.

diet.

Exercise alone can do nothing when you end up eating junk outside. I was a huge foodie, I must admit. I couldn't survive a day without at least two bigger packets of chips. And sweets, oh my god! I can't live without it. I still have a really sweet tooth.

And when it was time to give up on all my favourite foods, it was really a tough task for me. But, as I told you when your priorities are clear, you can do anything, to any point.

Honestly, I didn't quit everything. I had it during the process, and I still have it once in a while. But yes! definitely, I have reduced the amount as much as possible and also replaced all the unhealthy items with a healthy version of it as much as I could.

When it comes to food, I believe it's not about what you are eating. More, it's about how much you are eating. And after all, I believe, what is the meaning of having such a life when you can't even enjoy your favourite food even for once. So, I eat but definitely, fewer times.

And as I said, for me, I started with the thought that this is going to be my whole lifestyle shift, which means this will last forever. And food… These played as motivation to work even harder. Because trust me, when I plan my week and think that I will be going to have a cheat meal on Sunday. You know, the amount of motivation it gives me to work even harder is really huge. Because I work hard to get my favourite bar of chocolate, or my favourite black currant ice cream, or a peri-peri chicken pizza from Domino's, or crispy hot wings from KFC.

My idea of staying healthy and eating food is that you are allowed to have your food as long as it doesn't cost you your health. Obviously! Everything is important, health is all about balance.

Well, when I started with my diet, I meant a healthy diet. The best part of this is that I learned how to cook and the bonus point is, that it doesn't even taste awful. Because my family members praise me for my cooking. All thanks to my diet, I learned a life-saving skill.

Eight months down, I had lost 22kg, improved my sleep cycle, and changed my eating habits. I'm now able to wear clothing in a small size. And I love everything about it. But still, the best part of this process is that I cured my 12-year-old PCOS, which doctors said couldn't be cured. I increased my vitamin D level, which is now in the normal range. I got rid of my migraine; it no longer bothers me on alternate days like it used to. My thyroid was cured.

When you work hard and then get results for that, that is the best feeling in the world. Now, I don't have to have those kilos of medicine.

I am fit, healthy, and happier than ever. Because a healthy body gets you a healthy mind.

making it for them.

I was a very pampered child. I was the eldest child, so I was loved in the same way that I was being experimented with everything. Every parent does that for their children, I'm sure. That is special despite the fact that it has nothing special about it. There is uniqueness in expressing their love. Oh sorry, their unconditional love.

My parents have always given me and never asked me anything in return. Everything that I demand, they tried with all their capabilities. When I was firm with my decision to go to Visakhapatnam, I knew they took a loan for me, but they never let me know.

When I was in my graduation, it cost me Rupees 5000 a month, but they used to send me 10,000 a month. Not just in materialistic things, but whenever I was low, I don't know how they understand just by listening to my voice even though I tried my hardest possible to hide that.

And with no time, they try their hardest possible to make everything better. Sometimes, I feel they are just magicians. Well, yeah! Psychologists too.

Till the time I was staying in the hostel, I must say, I never had a very good relationship with my parents. Not good in the sense, not very close that I could spend hours and hours with them. I don't know, maybe I was away from them for more than seven years, so I think that might be one of the reasons that I used to feel more comfortable staying outside than at my home.

But then all thanks to this COVID-19 pandemic that has changed my entire life, including my relationship with my parents.

I have realized that the parents-children relationship is also a give-and-take kind of relationship. I was so selfish that sometimes, I didn't even have time to talk with my own parents. I could spend one hour talking to an unknown person, but with my own parents, I didn't even want to spend five minutes. This is really sad but my reality.

When I came back home, I saw my parents having trouble with their legs, their mood, their understanding, and everything else.

My dad's legs hurt when he walks for a bit longer. And my mom on the other side couldn't even walk for more than five minutes.

I feel they misinterpret everything. Sometimes, it takes a much longer time for them to understand a simple thing.

These are all normal things, but aren't these all signs of aging?

They are aging!

They are getting so much dependent on me and my brother for everything that we sometimes get scared of them.

They smile and assure us that they are all right. But I know, they need us, me and my brother.

We get busy growing up so much that we forget that our parents are growing old too. And when parents get old, they need their children's support.

It's not about returning a favor that they have done much for us so we need to do something for them back. It's about our responsibilities, our duty towards them.

Yes! They are the biggest gifts we have, and what else can

we offer other than spending time with them. I know, my parents would never have to depend upon us financially. All they require is support.

81

It will again be wrong to say, they will ever require… Because they deserve it.

living moments.

Live your every moment as if this is your last moment.

That's true! We should live every moment just like we love to live in our last moment.

We, humans, always live either with regrets or responsibilities. We spend our whole life after two questions, "Why" and "How". "Why did we do this?" and "How should we live our lives?

Have you realized that we spend our whole life after something that we can't change and the other that we don't even know? But through all these, we forget one precious thing… Our present. It's today that is in our control. We forget about that because we forget about living.

Life is too short to fill any regrets inside it. And too uncertain to predict the future. So, why not spend the right time with the right attitude towards it.

I have learned many lessons in these past years, but I believe this lesson is my favorite of all. I learned it when I had the worst emotional breakdowns and mental trauma during my M.Sc.

I learned that running after things that we can't even control is a waste of our time. And our time is the most precious gift of our life.

So, better invest your time wisely.

I ran after a person for five years who doesn't even deserve my time. But can I change anything now except wasting time again thinking about that and building up regrets around me? I can't! I can do nothing except waste time again. But do I want that again? No! Absolutely not! I can't afford any of my time spent on something that doesn't even deserve my time.

Well, when it comes to my performance in academia, I was always an average student. I failed the medical entrance test. I literally murdered all of my dreams. But can I change anything now? If I think about this too much, can I fix anything? No! I can't. I can never fix any of these.

My dad always says, "Time once lost, can't be regained." Absolutely! If we can't live our present wisely and to our fullest, it will be a regret for the rest of our life.

And talking about tomorrow, has anyone ever seen it? At least, I haven't seen my future. I can't even tell you about my very next moment. I can't tell whether I will sleep in the next moment, or I will be hungry, or whether I will feel like going out or spend time writing absolutely shit. No! Maybe I can do nothing about it or maybe something. Likewise, in life, I don't know where my life will take me to.

I don't know… Maybe I will be a big writer tomorrow… I can be a researcher… I can even be a famous designer… Or I will just marry and raise a family. I absolutely have no idea. But I know one thing, what can I do now? I know, I love to write, I know, I love to design and develop that design… I know how much I love insects and studying them… I know how much I am about zoology and research.

As long as I am happy with all of these, I will do it with neither any regret nor any expectations.
I believe in living my life to the fullest. After all,

84

Who knows, when a moment becomes a memory?

getting the hang of it.

attainment.

From the time I was born till the time I realized I am a failure, I did nothing but wasted my time and energy on things that are short-term. I was so busy making others happy that I almost forgot about my happiness, about my achievements.

Actually, when we move out with degrees in our hands, then the real struggle starts. It's the time when you realize, "Am I doing the right thing?" "What do I actually want to do?" "What do I want from my life?" "Who do I want to be?" And several things…

And the questioning itself is the most important part of the journey. Well, finding those answers is tougher than it may sound… But trust me once you find all the answers, the rest can be history.

The time when I figured out answers for all the questions, was the time when I realized, isn't it what exactly I wanted to do? Isn't it what I want to be?

I realized that I was walking on the path where there was no "me", there was "everybody". What do they do? What do they think? What to make them happy?

No! It's not the way things are intended to be. A person's life is entirely their own property. How can you expect to obtain the returns if you can't invest in your property? You and only you have power over your life and career; if you don't work to create a better life, trust me, no one else will! Self-investment means building a new road to several new opportunities. It means building confidence to pursue dreams, and opening doors for new opportunities. It does not just mean enriching a CV, it means enriching life with ideas, people, creativity, scope, hobbies, and several experiences. Self-investment is the greatest investment. Investing in self means, making small but continuous improvements, be it little but long-term happiness. Self-investment means, investment in one's own happiness.

Well, how to invest in yourself is also completely to the person searching for it. But because till that time, I was a failure. I failed at almost everything, everything that I desired, and everything that I looked up to, as a student, a friend, a daughter, a sister, and as a person. I was so busy setting up unrealistic goals for myself and running after things that I would never get to have, that I forgot about the things that I can achieve if I work for it like my health, my skills, my dreams, my hobbies, my relationships and everything else.

When I realized it, I started working for it. And in those two years, and following that, I have learned to invest in my greatest asset.

Now when someone asks me "What is your achievement to date?"

Well… I have an answer to that.

My self-investment is my greatest achievement.

stars of my

galaxy.

the stars, as they appear.

Well, thanksgiving is purely getting together with family, friends, and everybody else in this world. Everything and everybody that happened to date, deserves a "Thank You". Because I believe, every step forward is a step toward something bigger, and something better than the current one.

From my birth givers to the people I walked with to the people who made me walk, everyone is just more than worth acknowledging. All the people are not just behind the making of "Prickles and the bubbles", they are the ones behind me, behind the making of me.

Thanksgiving is not just enough because they deserve more than this. So, this is treasured of all. For the better and for the worse, I know I had them and I will have them, forever.

It is just a moment to cherish the bond, the relationship, the differences, the support, and all the thousands of beautiful moments I always looked up to and will look up to.

They are all who complete my galaxy.

Because they are the stars of my galaxy.

birth givers.

My parents are the biggest liars on this planet I have ever seen. I know they lie when they say they are proud of me.
I know, they can't be! How can parents be proud of a child who hasn't done anything for them, who always walks against the path they have shown, and who never followed them at any point in life? I wonder, how can parents be the best for the worst child. I think that's why they are called parents.
At times, actually, most of the time, it becomes very difficult for them to understand my choice, my ambitions, my career choice, and many more things. It becomes difficult for them to match the pace of today's world.
Just last time, when my first scientific paper got published, I was more than happy and they could see that. They grin! But not because they understood what a scientific paper means or what a scientific paper getting published means. I know they don't understand either of them. But still, they were happy because I was happy. I heard them saying "We are so proud of you."
They are proud not because I have done something of their choice or for them, it's because I have done something of my choice and because I was happy doing that.
They are not old, but yes! Definitely, one step behind getting things. Well, I understand that for them, everything is very new. Adaptation requires time, and so do they! I

know that to see through their eyes and understand what we are trying to convey is really tough for them.

It must not be actually easy for them to grow up in an environment that never made them aware of the things they are going through now. Coming from a small village in West Bengal, and then residing again in a small city, with no outside interactions, and then all of sudden a huge transformation, their actions, their thoughts… Everything is so different for them.

Actually, it's all the difference in time. Our parents come from a different era, a completely different time. It was the offline world, where everything was slow, where people used to write letters. The time when four o'clock in the evening means coming from school unlike now when people go to sleep at four in the morning. That time was so simple, yet extremely peaceful.

For them, simple things include being born, growing up, going to school, and college, and trying their luck in government job exams. Once you've found a job, the next step is to get married, have children, and raise a family. For them, life is simple, normal, and peaceful. They didn't know anything beyond this, and I doubt they still can think anything beyond this now.

Except for one… Parenting!

However, unlike us, they are unable to multitask. They could only do one thing at a time, and that was parenting. They were so involved in parenting that they almost forgot that while raising a child, parents should step outside of their role and become more of a friend. They forgot that parenting isn't complete unless there's friendship, a close bond between parent and child.

And I was a stupid, failed child that I couldn't understand how difficult it must be for them. I was that child who always misunderstood her parents' intentions behind things, the intentions behind their actions, and the intentions behind their thoughts.

I know, they are not perfect. They are not as flawless as we expect a person to be. They made mistakes, a lot of mistakes. Certainly, they are imperfect because they are just human creations. They are just human beings. And they are allowed to make mistakes as much as they are expected not to.

There are several things that they didn't allow me to do but yet they did many such great things for me. Well, as I said they are not perfect which means I am saying yes! They made mistakes, which are acceptable though. Because more than that I made mistakes to understand them every time. I made mistakes thinking my parents didn't understand me. I made mistakes yelling at them every time when they didn't agree with me at some point. I made mistakes blaming them for every bad experience I had in the past. I made mistakes in every single thing.

A few days back, when I was talking to one of my friends on WhatsApp after a really long time, she asked me "Where are you and what are you up to?" I said, "At home and a little involved with my Ph.D. application and other stuff." Then just as any normal person would do, I asked her back "What about you, what are you up to?" She said, "My parents have been forcing me to get married since 2016, it's been six years now so finally I said okay for it, so the process of a typical arranged marriage is going on, it's just the delay of the date getting fixed." I said, "Wow, congratulations!" She replied back "I wanted to study and stand up on my feet, but my parents didn't allow me to do it. Ekta, you are really lucky to have such supportive parents." That time I realized, Yes! Yes, obviously I am! I am really lucky to have such parents, in spite of all the things that they didn't allow me to do, they still allowed me to do many things… They allowed me to grow, they allowed me to fly.

Well, in my entire group of friends, I am the only one who is not married yet, the rest are married, and some of them have kids, and are raising families. I actually never thought about it before she said. Because I don't get bothered about marriage and all, and neither do my parents!

Really lucky!

Not just that, but in every decision, they agreed. Because they have faith in me, they believe me.

As children, we become so selfish sometimes. Sometimes we just look for our comfort, our things, our food, our clothes… These make us so busy that parents' millions of sacrifices are just overlooked.

It was the day when I came to know my parents had to ask for money from door to door so that I could get the best of all facilities so that I could make my dreams come true, but I failed. That day when I realized that my parents always buy me clothes for every festival and otherwise but for them, no festival could make them buy. It was the day when they called me several times just to make sure everything is good with me, and I was irritated with their multiple calls. It was the day when I came to know that all their intentions were so unintentional and I made the mistake of misunderstanding them. It was the day when I realized… I wanted to say something to them.

Dear Maa and Baba,

I remember you saying, "Once you become parents, you will understand everything". But now, I say, sometimes we do not even need to be one to understand someone's role. It just needs thinking, thinking from the other person's side. Can you believe, your daughter is too grown up to think about you, to understand you. And now as I understood, all I wanted to say to you are just two things, a sorry, and a thank you.

Sorry that I was really greedy to ask more from you, to seek more from you, to expect more from you. I am sorry for searching for a friend in you when I had the best of parents. Sorry that I had mistaken all your intentions behind whatever and whenever you did something or tried to do something for me. I am sorry that I wanted you to be there for me every time.

Trust me, I wanted to share everything, every single trauma which I had to face alone, but… I just couldn't because I thought, you would never understand me just like before.

But I think that's where I was hugely mistaken about your intentions. You went on pretending not to understand me while you were actually making me strong, allowing me to handle everything alone. You allowed me to make my own decisions. You let me fall because you knew that when I rise, I will shine brighter than before. Because you believe me, and your parenting. You let me grow and learn. You let me be me.

Well, I must tell you, you are a liar. You pretend to be strong when you actually aren't. You pretend to be okay when you are broken because I was low. You pretend to be okay when you cry even more because I cried.

At times, when I burst out at you, shout at you, I know you were hurt, you questioned your parenthood, a lot of times. I know you cried, blamed yourself too. But how simply you hid it from me, from everyone. I know that it wasn't that simple to smile over things that hurt you the most. I know you had to face as much as I had.

I never bothered to realize that you were just too lost in your parenthood, in raising me that you didn't notice any other things in life. I am sorry that I expected you to be flawless, I forgot that you are human too, and parents later. You are free to make mistakes even as parents. I know you were, are, and you always will be my well-wisher.

I know I am the kind of daughter that a parent might not want to have but you are those parents that every kid would want to have.

I understand, at times you aspire to have my support too. Sometimes, when you ask me for anything, to give my point of view on matters which you could solve yourself too, I really feel proud. But you know, sometimes when you ask me to teach you how to make an order online, how to use Flipkart or Myntra or even Amazon, and yes! When you want me to teach you how to update a status on WhatsApp and I simply say try that yourself, don't come to me. Trust me, I want to teach you everything. I do have time to take you out for you, but I just don't want to.

Because I want you to be the strongest of all. To learn by yourself and not depend on anyone else. I wanted you to learn, to grow just the way you wanted for me. And the person I know as my parents, as independent, strong, and the most tolerant of all, I want you to be the same, always! You don't even have any idea how much your dependency makes me freak out. I get afraid that while I am growing up, you are growing old too. While I am aging, you are aging too. Now is not forever. Many things have changed, and many will be, it's just our bond, the time we spend together will remain the same, forever!I know, I lost many such times spent with you, and cherish them forever. I wish I could have understood you and all your intentions behind everything. I wish I would not just waste my entire childhood blaming you for everything. I just wish I could have accepted you just the way you are.

I wish… I wish I could change all the differences between you and me, I can't.

But now, not anymore. Because now is the time. So, I want to tell you what I never told you before, about what important role you play in my life. I never told you how important you are in my life. I never told you that I love you. Because I failed. I fail sometimes, to express my love for you, I fail to show my love for you. But that doesn't mean I don't love you. I just want you to know that you are that precious thing in my life, that I am afraid of losing. I am sorry for all the pain that you had to walk through for me. And thank you for making me as I am!

Yours'

Not so ideal daughter

the person i grew up with.

My brother is the person I grew up with. Although we have an age gap of ten years, which means when he was born, I already lived ten years of my life but I actually grew up with him, not only by age, but also by maturity, thoughts, and openness.

I know, this might sound a bit strange but the reality is, that he is the actual person behind me. All the acuity in my vision, the break of two years, and then again rising and shining brighter than before, whatever I could do… Everything is just because of him.

Just because of that one night, that one hour of conversation with him, his just one question, "What do you actually want to do?" Honestly, I could see not just a concerned brother asking her sister what she wants to do, but also a friend who is just curious about his friend's plans for the future.

Honestly, I think I needed that. Because in that entire one hour, we were two open books and still couldn't get enough of it. It's all because of that one hour of our conversation, and his precious suggestions, I found myself with a clear vision and a different perspective on my life.

Well, I have to say, we didn't have a great childhood together. As I said, we have an age gap of ten years. So, when he turned six, I was done with my 10th board and then I had to shift to a hostel, and then I kept traveling from one place to another for my studies further. But until he turned six and I was at home, I was the one who was always jealous of him.

Actually, when you get extra care, extra pampering, extra love from everyone for ten years, and then all of sudden someone else becomes the center of attraction, all the affection. This fact was actually tough to accept for me. Although I was a grown-up but was still a kid to understand such things.

But yes! This didn't mean that I never loved him. I loved him as much as everyone else loved. But the only thing was... Me. I started feeling unloved. I started feeling left out.

In many ways, he had far superior facilities to me. Better environment, better education, better friends, better experiences, and, of course, better parents. Yes! I'm referring to their understanding, as they are now experienced.

The mistakes that you make on your first trial, don't repeat the second time, right? I was always the lab rat, and my brother got the filtered ones, he got to experience the results, not experiment.

In fact, I was given a cellphone during my graduation, and... He got his cellphone when he was eight.

So unfair to me!

I feel bad for him as much as for me. I feel bad that he deserved a sister's love, a pure love, but my complexities overshadowed that. I feel bad that all he needed was a friend in me when I was busy counting our differences. I feel bad that I couldn't give him a memorable childhood that he can cherish forever. I feel even worse than...

I was so wrong about him! I was looking through a different eye to the situation. I was so wrong comparing us. I was so wrong not to understand that we two are two individuals, with two identities, two individuality, and two circumstances.

Everything changes with time and so do people! And everything becomes better with maturity and so does parenting, the reason why he got a better understanding of parents so early in his life. The time when I was budding off, was a transition era when technologies were shifting towards their advanced stage. I was not exposed to the internet, or tech world, or any tech advancements, but my brother does! He is better exposed to everything very early in his life and so, he needed a cellphone to match the pace of the World.

The two different worlds, the two different persons, and the two different identities can never be compared. Be it, siblings, be it, friends, be it, neighbors, be it anyone else in the world. But here I made a mistake again. And this was one of the biggest mistakes I have made in my life, I know. I always compared both of us. This was the center of attraction for everyone to the fact that he was already doing great towards his goals, so early in his life. Within two years of the cell phone being given to him, he proved to everyone why he is worth having the one.

Unlike me, he didn't waste time running after things that can drive him to waste his time, he focused on utilizing his time, and proved everyone wrong that a child can do a lot more things with a cellphone than only waste time on social media and other kinds of stuff.

No one knew that he was into exploring his life. Even I yelled at him several times when I found him always busy doing something with his cell phone. But the day when he paid the bill for our entire shopping, that moment was really shocking for us, all of us!

I remember my dad calling and asking me, "Beta, what is he doing with his mobile? I don't know, all I want to know is, is it legal?" I laughed at my dad's innocent question, but I said "Dad, don't you trust your upbringing?" Then I asked him every detail of his work, and his source of having money in his account. I don't know how, but he explained it to me this time. Well, I was so happy for him to hear that my little brother is not little anymore. He can pay bills now.

I was still not convinced about improving the bond and all the differences between us. It was still more formal than a friendship.

But then a day arrives in my M.Sc. when I was more than frustrated with my life. I was lost in the world, with no close person to share any bit of what I was going through. I wasn't performing well in my academics. I started losing myself and my parents and my brother were going out to Puri. I already knew about that. But still, when they called me on their way to Puri, I burst on them. I yelled at every one of them, my mom, my dad, and my brother too.

I know, I shouldn't do that. But I was very bad at controlling my anger. I put all of them into a different situation where neither they could draw an idea of how to calm me nor they could enjoy their trip.

My brother called me again sometimes after I cut the first call yelling at them. I received and was almost about to yell at him again, but I stopped! He said something before I would say anything. He said, "I know you are low." "So, tell me what happened?"

I knew this was not that little boy, not a brother asking his sister about what happened and why the hell I yelled at everyone. This was more mature, calmer, and a genuine friend who is just curious about knowing his friend, and what happened to her.

I told him every detail about why this happened. I told him that I failed my biochemistry paper in my class and just couldn't handle that because I was so clueless that I didn't even have any idea how to deal with any more failures. And I couldn't tell my parents about any more failures because they expect much more than I expect from myself, they trust the abilities that I could ever trust about myself.

The entire time, he listened to me quietly, and then when I stopped, he said, "I know there is more. I know, my sister just can't cry upon such tiny things. I know, my sister is the strongest person who works through everything, who is childish yet mature, she is all in one."

I wondered more than I cried, how can a little boy say such mature things? How does he already know what exactly I needed?

And that was the moment, I cried more over everything, more than what I did to him, more that I was a failed sister, more that I couldn't be there for him when he needed me, more that I couldn't provide him a friendly environment around him. And there was more... I couldn't help but cry.

Now, that's it! Something had to end now to start something new. Our bond.

After that night, everything changed, everything between us. And I could say, we are more than just siblings, friends.

After that, I tried every possible thing to make everything friendly between me and him.

From personal to professional lives, our conversation time gradually increased. We started sharing every single detail about our lives, about every day. And slowly, everything between us started to be better.

And we started knowing each other better, actually more than anyone can understand. And each day, I learned from him how to be a good person. How to work through things, what to see and what not to see, what has to stop and whatnot, everything.

The more I started understanding him, the more I got to know his other side. He never failed to surprise me with his thoughts, ideas, maturity, and responsibilities. And yes not to forget all the surprises…

I don't understand how he could understand what I need at the moment. I needed to purchase an earphone but I forgot to tell you that at home. Then after a few days, I received a message. The message was saying, I had to collect a parcel from my university main gate. I was surprised because as far as I remember, I didn't order anything for myself, then who did?

Well, I rushed to the main gate as soon as my classes were over and received the parcel. I couldn't hold my excitement about opening it and seeing what was inside that. As soon as I reached my room, I tore the wrap and saw that it was a wireless Bluetooth earphone, exactly what I desired, exactly what I required.

I immediately received a call from my brother, he said, "How is it like?" "How did you like your earphones?" Man! I can't even explain how happy I was. If there were no one inside my room, I could probably jump with excitement, I was that happy.

How does he understand me and all my needs before I even tell him? And I don't know how a person can surprise someone every time. Because I haven't seen anyone like that. My surprise was just one call away. I just needed to call and say, "I am hungry." He knows exactly what I like to eat. And even if I tell him, I feel like eating a pizza, the order has already been placed and I knew, it will never be just a pizza. There will be something, what I call surprise. He knows exactly how I like to eat pizza, with a coke and a choco lava cake.

And yes! This was one of the reasons why I gained so much weight. But yes! I liked it that way. Because as much as he made me gain weight, he helped me lose weight too.

When I started my weight loss journey and every second felt like now enough, I couldn't get through it. I found him to hold me, to support me, and to motivate me throughout the process. He even started working out with me so that I don't feel out of motivation. He sacrificed his work and took out time for me just to keep me motivated, just to get my results. I know that no words can justify his support for me. He is more than the gratitude I can show towards him.

Not just that but while pursuing my interests, whether it is designing, developing, or writing, he helped me throughout, and he motivated me every time, every moment.

When I said, "I want to write a book." He was more than happy. He said, "Go for it and let me know if you need any help in writing." I said, "I am just afraid, what if no one reads my book." He said, "Even if no one reads it, I will order 100s of your copies and read it a thousand times."

How? How can a person motivate me so well? How does he know me so well?

Well…

Hey Bruh,

For a long time, I wanted to say so many things to you, but couldn't. Do you want to know why? Wait, I will tell you. Because after all, we are siblings, man! And siblings don't say any good things about each other, just like I never said that "Yes! You are my best friend." I never said that "I feel the luckiest to have you in my life." I never said that "I was nowhere in the queue and you made me stand at least somewhere."

Well, when it is all about accepting things then yes! I have to accept that I was the one with no clarity of goals, you made me wear the glasses to see through it. I have to accept that when I had to go through multiple rejections, you felt defeated, more than I. I have to accept that when I cry for some reason, you cry for one reason I cried. I have to accept that when we both go to market and walk on the road, you walk on my right making sure I am safe. I have to accept that you hate waiting but you can simply wait for hours outside the parlor because you can't leave me alone there. I have to accept that when I was grinning at my small achievements, all the frontends, how simply you hide facts that you handled the whole backend, all the bigger responsibilities so well.

I have to accept that when I was at my lowest, you were the one to push me up. I have to accept that when no one else believed in me, you were the one standing beside me, believing me. I have to accept that whenever I am happy, you are more than happy, happier than me.

Today if I could write this, then the reason has to be you, because of your faith, your belief in my abilities. Because you believed that I could do it and see, I did!

And there is more that I want to tell you. More than I wish I could have given you the childhood that you deserved. I wish I could be your friend when you needed that. I wish I just didn't waste my entire childhood creating differences between you and me. I wish I could not just have compared both of us. I wish I could just have understood you when you needed that. I wish I could be you…

For the better and for the worse, I know I have the best of all. The best brother on this entire planet, who will be standing beside me even if the whole world gets against me. I know I have the best teacher in my life who never fails to teach me lessons. I know I have a beautiful soul, because I know I have you.

Thank you so much for growing up with me. And you know what? When I grow up, I wanna be you!

Keep swimming…

Wait! We will keep swimming until we reach our shores!

Your

Not so best sister

the people who proved me wrong.

Friendship…
Isn't it the most beautiful word in the dictionary? It says, friendship is a mutual affection between people. Yes! Mutual… But my previous experience with friends was just something I am not very proud of.
Well, maturity is the term that grows with us. I believe maturity makes everything better, understanding, trust, clarity, relationships, and friendships too. And I think that was one of the reasons why I had some previous bad experiences with friends. Because we weren't wrong, but our maturity was. We were not at the moment where we understood what friendship means and what friends are meant for.
The bad experiences have the power to change a person's way of looking at the world, to things. I believed that I could never have a friend in my life. I believed not to believe anyone else outside the family. It was the time when I met three beautiful souls at different places, at different times, and with different expectations. They are the ones who made me realize that no! Not all are the same. This is all because of them that I found a different definition of friendship.
They made me realize friendship is not something where you expect something from the other person. It is so mutual that you don't have to expect anything and everything just happens. They made me realize that

friendship is the purest bond anyone can have. It's so pure and weird that the people who were just unknown someday become so close that you don't even have a second thought of doing something together. It is absolutely pure, innocent, and obviously, beautiful. I believe that's why it's called family away from family.

When I went to the hostel, away from my family to stay there and complete my graduation in Ranchi, the first person I met was Vijeta who was my roommate and classmate. We didn't have anything in common, we come from two entirely different worlds. And just a thin string that kept us together was our understanding. She was a bit conservative where I was her exact opposite pole, very open about everything. But our understanding overshadowed every difference in between.

I remember when I failed the selection test and I was worried, it was Vijeta who brought a plan when she saw my face and teary eyes. She said, "Let's lie about your marks when any other roommate asks about it." Well, that worked! Because I was worried about how to face roommates and family more than the fact that I was not performing well. It was her who cheered my mood every time I was low. And about my writing skills, I must say, she had a great initiative in it so that later on, my scores actually started improving.

From sharing about absolute shit to sharing about family matters, we actually developed a great bond.

When I talk about Ranchi, definitely, I talk about memories, but more than that I talk about people with whom I could make memories. And among them, Vijeta and Archana are two kinds. We have countless memories, memories of individuals, and memories in common.

Archana is the sweetest of all, the sweetest person I have ever met in my life. Well, we met her in college and it's been eight years, she is exactly the same the way she was on the first day we met. Sometimes I wonder how a person can be this difficult to change.

I still remember our first conversation, that is because it was very awkward and we still laugh when we talk about that. When we talked, it was two seconds of talk and another two hours of awkward silence. But soon, our two seconds started turning into 20, 30, 40, 50 minutes, then one hour. And now, when we talk, it is only talking with no scope of silence. We grew up together and so did our friendship. Not just in college but outside the college, we made a great team, a great bond, and a great friendship.

I am still figuring out why all my friends are vegetarian when I am a huge chicken lover. Well, that's okay! But for them, I have to eat vegetarian foods. And fine, I can do that, there is no big deal. But it is a big deal when my pure vegetarian friend takes me to a non-vegetarian restaurant and just lets me eat what I love the most.

Well, I am talking about my friend Archana, she is a pure vegetarian. But when I say I feel like eating outside, every time she takes me to KFC... Man! She knows me very well. I don't have to tell her when I say something, what does that actually mean. I know she understands, and she does it so perfectly that when I had an emotional breakdown following our graduation studies, she was the one to come to my hostel the very next day in the morning just to make sure I am okay! And the whole day, we just roamed around and ate all our favorites. Because she knows exactly how my mood gets lifted.

Be it 2 P.M. in the afternoon or 2 A.M. at night, she was, she is, and I believe, she will always be there for me. Because this girl is too difficult to change, I know. We know all the secrets about each other, and even more than that we know each other very well and so does our long-distance friendship.

Talking about long-distance, when I went for my master's in Punjab, I met Ashu. I still remember, whenever we crossed each other, we used to smile; kind of formalities. And we came to know about each other more through a project in which we were assigned to work in a group, which was the time when I came to know we both were staying in the same hostel. Then after the first semester, we were to go home for winter vacation, and the people with whom I used to talk a lot, and sit together in class left for their homes already.

I clicked, and Ashu was there. I called her and asked her to go out the day before we were to leave for our homes. She agreed. We went out, had fun, spent the whole day, and the rest is history. That was the first time we went out, and after that, every Sunday meant an outing day for the two of us.

We had 9:00 A.M. to 5:00 P.M. classes and I still don't know how we used to get that patience after eight hours of hectic classes to go out for pasta or sandwich and a coke, sitting at our favorite place, judging people together and spending hours talking about life, until it's time for hostel entry? Our frequent conversations, meetings, outings, and spending time with each other made us know about each other, and understand a bit more about each other. We shared our past lives because we two never had a fear of judgment. I remember, when we did, we were sitting at a park inside the campus, spending around 3.5 hours, and I talked everything about myself, and she did it too. And that conversation made us know even better, but yes! Without judgment.

Following my master's I had a huge mental trauma, which she knew everything about. So, that morning, we had to attend classes but I was not in the mood to attend, she said "let's go out and sit there". And didn't realize, we already missed one class. I was talking, and just crying in front of her. She hugged me, and now for the next class, I told her that I won't be able to attend it because I feel like going to the hostel and taking a rest. "Okay! Let's not attend classes today, let's go to a counselor "Even if you told me everything, sometimes you need a professional to handle it," she said. I realized I have another gem of a person.

Be it Vijeta, Archana, or Ashu, not just in helping out or supporting, I know, our friendship is more than that. These three are the three gems of a person, three different individuals.

We all want different things in our lives, we have grown up into different individuals, and our lives have changed, but our friendship is still the same. I know, we don't talk much now, everyone is busy figuring out their own lives, but still, whenever we talk, we don't have any scope of the void, silence, and expectations, because we understand each other, because we… Are friends.

As I said, you can never know what your future holds. Just like I didn't know at the time when I believed I would never find a friend. When I believed that making friends is the toughest task, I found three gems of people who made me realize that no! The toughest task is carrying the friendship more than making one.

I have come across several people in life, before these three and after them. There are several who claim to be friends but I know they are not. The real ones are just true ones, the honest ones.

I know, I don't have several friends. Because certainly, I have learned to choose quality over quantity.

people who helped me shine brighter.

When a baby is sent to school, parents believe that their kid would be learning something. The belief that parents do, is not on school, it's for the people in the school. It's the teachers who are there to guide their kids. The teachers that play very important roles in life, the teachers that make the real stars, the teachers that help their stars to shine brighter than before.

They are inspirations, for now, in the past, and for our whole life. As I said, I traveled from one place to another throughout my academia, and obviously! I came across more teachers than I could even count. And everyone has some impact on my life but among them, the five are the most important of all. These five are the ones that had a real impact on my life. They are the greatest source of my inspiration, for now, and forever.

Amongst them, my first inspiration was waiting for me in my class 9th when I was struggling with my English, and when I was insulted by my parents. Ms. Poornima, our class teacher, English teacher, and alongside she also used to teach the Oriya language to the students.

She was the first person to make me believe that it's never late to start over again. I can do it, and I can do it again. She was the inspiration that I started working on my English and on my scores when I barely could manage to pass. As much as she helped me develop an interest in studies, she made sure I stayed motivated.

I remember with the best of my memories, that it was the first day of our school. "Roll No. 51", she called. Yeah! I was roll number 51. Surprisingly, in the whole class, she asked me to introduce myself. This was something I had never done before, still, I tried, and as I started "I'm Ekta Bera…" "It's okay, sit", she stopped me in the middle. I thought I must have said something wrong. I was worried about my impression in front of her, which I might have ruined at first. But afterwards, she was the one looking for me every time she entered the class. Lately, I became the most interactive student in the whole class. And that's how I didn't even realize that I was actually developing an interest in studies.

I still remember the time of our class 9th exams. It was our English Exam and I was sitting with other students who were not from my class and some other invigilator was assigned for that room. Well, as I started writing my paper and was completely on to it, I didn't realize who was coming in or going out of the classroom. "I want you to score more than 80 marks this time", I heard something like that. As I looked up, there she was, our class teacher. I smiled and replied, "I am trying ma'am". She said again "Not try, you have to, and I know you can do it".

The best part is that I realized that I don't have to be a good student, I have to be hard-working. However, I scored 86 marks on that paper. Not bad! And then after some days, we were called for a result announcement in our classroom. "Where is she?" Poornima ma'am asked. The whole class was looking at me, as they all knew, that if it is Poornima ma'am then she will always ask for Ekta in the class. "Class, meet our roll number 1," she said. The whole class was clapping and congratulating me. I was still processing what she just said, and what was just happening around my classroom. I couldn't believe it. I guess that was one of the happy days of my life.

And that motivation was so powerful that I started and never looked back. Obviously, the road was not at all easy. I walked, I failed, I was hurt, I cried, but I woke up again. Because I knew I had to do it. And that's how I made it to my class 11th admission. Being a Hindi medium student, I was completely exotic to that environment. I didn't only work on my academics, but also to survive in a different state, where the only means of communication was English. But you know what? I made it.

And then another failure that tore me apart, my dream broke down into pieces. And I was completely defeated. But the best part of failure is that you get to find other 999 ways to make things work for you. But yes! You need the right motivation for that. I found my way to make it up to Zoology.

Now college days have started…

A bit more excitement, a bit of nervousness, and unlimited memories were waiting on my way.

It was our first day at college, and after our freshman orientation in the auditorium, we had to report to our courses. When my friend, Vijeta and I, arrived at our department, neither of us was sure which room we had to sit in. I don't know what happened, I took a step forward, went to our department's staff room, and asked one of the ladies sitting over there, "Ma'am, Which room should we sit in?" She replied, "The next room that is attached to the staff room." I said, "Thank you, ma'am".

Then after 10-15 minutes of sitting inside that room, the same lady entered our class "Hello class, I am Dr. Emma, your HoD, I will be teaching and assisting you in your practical of first-year" she said. Man! She is our HoD. I was more than nervous! She started calling roll numbers for attendance and introduction.

She started with the very basic lesson "Taxonomy and classification", where we had to study the various classification of organisms and their naming. As she was moving with the chapter, she made her first question to the class "So, tell me who is considered the father of taxonomy?" "Carolus Linnaeus", I replied, because no one else was answering and secondly it was an easy one. "What's your name?" she asked me. I answered "Ekta Bera" and then she again asked me about my address and my educational background.

"First impression is the last impression", as they say; because after that day, there was not a single day, she questioned and I didn't answer that. Sometimes, after questioning, she used to ask me not to answer at first, "Let others speak on it." But when no one does, she'd say, "Answer Ekta."

It was the most beautiful feeling for me at that time to see the teacher expecting something from me. Isn't that what every student asks for? At least I do. My first day in college was more about making good impressions in front of every one of them. Not only in our HoD's class but in the other three teachers, Anjali Ma'am, Veena Ma'am, and Manisha Ma'ams' class, I was the most interactive that I have to agree with.

I remember, on the day of our first-year result, Manisha Ma'am was asking everyone about their marks scored. When it was my turn, I answered with a numb voice "69 percent". "Where is that 1%?", she said to me. I realized, why did she say that to me? In front of the whole class where she didn't say a single word to anyone, why me? I realized one thing: she had expected from me.

Two years down, and it was our final year, we had a project to do under the supervision of a teacher. Well, that was a really great opportunity for me and for all the students to know their supervisors in a better way. And I had a chance to work under Veena Ma'am. I knew she was the sweetest of all, but through that project, I came to know her supportive side even more. Not something very new! But still, it is an absolute pleasure knowing her.

Everybody was supportive in our department, but as far as Veena ma'am is concerned, she is somewhere a bit on the more side of the scale. She not only guided me about the procedure of performing tasks but also helped me use every piece of equipment that I was supposed to use. Her sweetness created a really comfortable zone around her between her and us, so not a single student hesitated to approach her anytime at any point. Whenever I had any doubt, no matter what the topic is all about, I never hesitate to ask her, be it after two years or after 7 years, she never made me return empty-handed. Even though she doesn't have an answer, she always has a suggestion, a direction as to where to find your perfect answer.

Just last time, when I needed help in selecting a topic for my Ph.D. I was very confused, I had many questions in my mind. And then one person came into my mind, who can resolve all of my doubts, that's Veena ma'am. I messaged her. It was after 2 or 3 years that I messaged her. But still, she didn't even make me realize that we had no conversation for a long time. She suggested I talk to Anjali ma'am as she has abundant knowledge about the research field. As per her directions, I talked to Anjali ma'am, and I found answers to all of my questions.

As much as Veena ma'am is supportive, Anjali ma'am is caring too. She is a great personality, strong outside, and damn emotional inside.

I still remember Anjali ma'am once saying, "You guys won't get it now, once you won't have anyone to nag you, the moment you will realize why we always keep telling you about things". And that's true, we didn't realize it when she was saying, we just said, she has a great thought, but the meaning of it, we have learned after we left college when we had to live a life outside our four walls when we had to survive through the pollution of this World, and by the time we had no one, to suggest us, to tell us what to do, where to go, how to do, and a lot more things.

One day, after our final year results, my friends went to college for some paperwork. As I was walking through the corridor, I heard a voice "Ekta, come here." That's Anjali ma'am sitting in the staff room. I took my steps toward her, "Yes ma'am you were calling me." She said "You know Ekta, I know your marks do matter for you now, but it won't for the long term, doesn't matter whether you get some lesser marks or some more marks, it will always be you and your hard work that will remain with you. I know you are very hard working. Never lose that, never lose yourself." And that's one of the reasons why I always say Anjali ma'am is the greatest source of inspiration in my life.

And why not? She didn't say a word to all the other 41 students in our class, then why only me? I realized that people tell them who they expect something from. And expectations don't come from anything, but from a relationship, a bond. And I knew, I created a great bond with all of them. Otherwise, which teacher can recognize a student even after five years of no contact. No one does!

All the four ladies of our Zoology family are the pillars. Not only during the time when we were studying there but beyond that, at any point of the time. Sometimes we don't even know what impact we are creating around us, just like them. They are such a gem of a person that even they are not aware of it.

I really admire how they balance their personal life and professional life. They are the perfect example of superwoman. I always look up to them. In every aspect, they are just perfect. I know, above all they are human too, and it's natural for them to have some other problems, but they never let reflect on their professional life.

I remember once Veena Ma'am telling us, "Choose your profession wisely so that you can maintain a balance between your personal and professional lives." And no surprises, why they never fail to amaze me. Being a daughter, a daughter-in-law, a sister, a sister-in-law, a wife, a mother, a teacher, and a lot more roles, with a lot more responsibilities. All the responsibilities come from all the tasks.

I have seen their gloomy faces when even after their immense efforts, a student fails. That reflects their dedication to their responsibility. I have seen them happy when we are happy. Those responsibilities, their performance, and their support are something that inspires me a lot, inspiring me not just to be a good student, but to be a good human being, and to be good in everything.

It's been seven years already, and I still remember my first interaction with all of them. I wonder why? Why do I still remember them? Why do I remember every small talk with them, everything that they had told me? Why do I always rush to them whenever I get stuck? Why do I never hesitate to contact them even after a huge time gap? Then I found an answer… That, you can never forget your inspirations, the people who have played a role in making you, the people who have helped you shine brighter and brighter and brighter, *the people who made you a star.*

Closure

closing

Umm… Now you know me very well. And we haven't even met yet. But I know, I will get to have you one day. And I just can't wait to hear about your story, all about your experiences, your failures, and successes.
Love,
Your homie

9 789356 107724